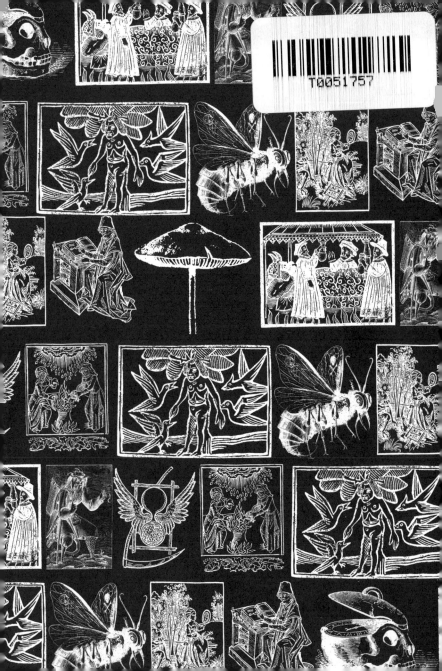

KITCHEN WITCH

NATURAL REMEDIES and CRAFTS for HOME, HEALTH, and BEAUTY

KATIE HAEGELE and NADINE SCHNEIDER

Microcosm Publishing
Portland, Ore

KITCHEN WITCH: NATURAL REMEDIES and CRAFTS for HOME, HEALTH, and BEAUTY

© 2021 Katie Haegele and Nadine Schneider
© This edition Microcosm Publishing 2021
First edition - 3,000 copies - March 23, 2021
ISBN 9781648410413
This is Microcosm #560
Cover by Lindsey Cleworth
Edited by Lydia Rogue
Design by Joe Biel

To join the ranks of high-class stores that feature Microcosm titles, talk to your local rep: In the U.S. **COMO** (Atlantic), **FUJII** (Midwest), **BOOK TRAVELERS WEST** (Pacific), **TURNAROUND** (Europe), **UTP/MANDA** (Canada), **NEW SOUTH** (Australia/ New Zealand), **GPS** in Asia, Africa, India, South America, and other countries, or **FAIRE** in the gift market.

For a catalog, write or visit:
Microcosm Publishing
2752 N Williams Ave.
Portland, OR 97227
https://microcosm.pub/KitchenWitch

Did you know that you can buy our books directly from us at sliding scale rates? Support a small, independent publisher and pay less than Amazon's price at **www.Microcosm.Pub**

Library of Congress Cataloging-in-Publication Data

Control Number: 2021034541

Global labor conditions are bad, and our roots in industrial Cleveland in the 70s and 80s made us appreciate the need to treat workers right. Therefore, our books are MADE IN THE USA.

MICROCOSM·PUBLISHING

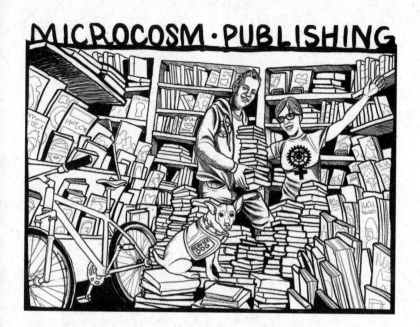

MICROCOSM PUBLISHING is Portland's most diversified publishing house and distributor with a focus on the colorful, authentic, and empowering. Our books and zines have put your power in your hands since 1996, equipping readers to make positive changes in their lives and in the world around them. Microcosm emphasizes skill-building, showing hidden histories, and fostering creativity through challenging conventional publishing wisdom with books and bookettes about DIY skills, food, bicycling, gender, self-care, and social justice. What was once a distro and record label was started by Joe Biel in his bedroom and has become among the oldest independent publishing houses in Portland, OR. We are a politically moderate, centrist publisher in a world that has inched to the right for the past 80 years.

CONTENTS

SECTION 1: WELCOME TO OUR KITCHEN

Introduction 9

Healing the World: Natural Living, Magic, and Community 11

A Word About Magic 11

A Brief History of Natural Healing 12

What Makes This Relevant Today? 16

Creating Community 19

The Well-Stocked Cupboard 21

Equipment and Ingredients 21

Essential Oils 29

Hydrosols 33

Aromatherapy 38

Preparation, Clean-Up, and Storage 40

Techniques and Conversions 44

Double Boiler 44

Solubilization 44

Infusions, Tinctures, and Decoctions 45

Distilled Water 50

Keeping a Grimoire 53

SECTION 2: CLEANING HOUSE

Introduction 57

One-Ingredient Wizardry 59

Lovely Liquid Laundry Soap 65

"It's About Thyme" Countertop Cleaner 67

Peppermint Pest Control 70

Bathroom Brightening Scrub 72

"Winter Woods" Room Spray 75

SECTION 3: WITCHY CRAFTS

Knit a Dishcloth 80

Wool Dryer Balls and Pet Toys 83

"Keep Out the Cold" Draft Stopper 87

Herbal Furniture Freshener 89

Dye Fabric the Natural Way 91

Make a Seasonal Wreath 94

Mind Your Beeswax 98

SECTION 4: IN THE GARDEN

Growing, Harvesting, and Preserving Herbs 110

Easy Household Composting 122

Citronella Mosquito Repellent 127

Air Purifying Houseplants 130

Into the Wild: A Note on Foraging 133

Creating a Backyard Wildlife Sanctuary 135

SECTION 5: HOLISTIC SELF-CARE

Introduction 143

Remedies for Skin and Hair 146

Everyday Rituals 171

CONCLUSION 177

ANNOTATED BIBLIOGRAPHY 179

RESOURCES 186

CREDITS 188

ABOUT US 189

Introduction

*H*ello, and welcome to the *Kitchen Witch: Natural Remedies and Crafts for Home, Health, and Beauty*! We're so glad you're here. Our names are Nadine and Katie, and we've known each other for several years now, ever since we started meeting for coffee in the break room at the university research center where we worked together. We soon became close friends, bonding over conversations about books, feminism, the 90s, and magic.

In 2016 we made a zine called "The Kytchyn Witche Guide to Natural Living" about one of our shared passions: natural remedies. Nadine, who has long been interested in natural skin and hair care, provided the recipes in the personal care section. Katie, an herb lover and enthusiastic house cleaner, gave instructions on how to make nontoxic cleaning supplies. After we finished writing we sat down at Katie's kitchen table to design and lay out the zine. We decorated the cover with medieval woodcuts of herbs and the moon, then started brainstorming titles. What should we call this collection of tips on natural living? Nadine got a faraway look, remembering something from her German childhood. A few Google searches turned it up: the kitchen witch! Created to look like a fairy tale witch, these little dolls are kept in the kitchen as good luck charms. No one knows exactly where this folk tradition originated, but it was most likely Northern Europe. We found the words "kytchyn witche" in an article that quoted an Englishman's will, dated 1599. The Elizabethan spelling had a certain charm, evoking the world of

Shakespeare with all its witches, apothecaries, and herbal lore. The name of our zine was born. It ended up being more popular than we ever expected, and two years later, the folks at Microcosm Publishing asked us to expand our ideas in order to make this beautiful book.

In thinking about what we wanted the *Kitchen Witch* book to be, we spent months tinkering and experimenting, testing our recipes and perfecting them. We collected tips from our mothers, other family members, and friends. We gathered together piles of books on herbal healing and plant magic and gleefully rolled around on the floor with them. (And yes, we read them, too.) In short, we've gained some knowledge, and we're happy and honored to be able to share it with you in these pages.

Healing the World: Natural Living, Magic, and Community

Kitchen witchery is the practice of making useful products for the home and body using common household equipment and simple, natural ingredients. We consider an ingredient to be natural when it comes directly from nature or has been minimally processed. Dried herbs, essential oils, and a few food pantry staples can all be found in a kitchen witch's cupboard.

Natural living is a lifestyle that honors nature and incorporates it into everyday life. This entails being mindful of our impact on the environment and actively nurturing our connection to the Earth. It doesn't mean being "perfect." For us, it means that we choose alternatives to plastic whenever possible, we try to avoid buying goods with excessive packaging (trust us, we know it's not easy), and we shop at thrift stores for secondhand items. We compost as much of our kitchen waste as we can, grow useful herbs and pollinator-friendly plants in our gardens, and celebrate the changing of the seasons.

A Word About Magic

Magic belongs to no one culture, society, or tribe—it is part of the universal wisdom.

–Laurie Cabot, *Power of the Witch*

What exactly is a kitchen witch? The term conjures up the image of an apron-clad homemaker casting spells over the stove with a wooden spoon. Although she is more interested in the domestic arts than the Dark Arts, she does dabble in magic. We love this portrait of a kitchen witch, but magic is not at all required in order to practice kitchen witchery and natural living. To us, it's all on a spectrum. At one end is pure practicality (the archetypal no-nonsense homemaker), and at the opposite end, Witchcraft practiced as religion (the archetypal Witch). There's plenty of room between the two for fostering a spiritual connection to nature, elevating everyday routines to rituals performed with intention, working with tarot cards and crystals, and casting spells only on holidays or for very specific purposes. In this book we mostly cover the practical aspects of kitchen witchery. We'll let you bring the magic.

A Brief History of Natural Healing

The mystical aspect of nature-based religions, on the surface of it, may seem pretty far removed from the practical use of plants for healing—but in a historical sense, the two ideas are inseparable.

Whether or not we call its practitioners witches, natural healing has a very long history. Written evidence of herbal remedies dates back 5,000 years to the ancient Sumerians, and archaeological evidence shows that plants were used as medicine 60,000 years ago, during the Paleolithic Age. We also know that in ancient and medieval Europe, most of these practioners were women: "wise women" who used folk medicine to treat illness, promote wellness, attend at childbirth, and perform abortions. This healing was considered a form of magic, and through the early middle ages, it was accepted and widely used. But beginning in the fourteenth century, both the use of charms (known as "superstitious magic") as well as the use of plants or animals as medicine or for protection ("natural magic") were considered oppositional to Christianity and therefore evil.

In their famous 1973 article "Witches, Midwives, and Nurses," Barbara Ehrenreich and Deirdre English wrote that the Catholic Church tried to destroy not only the witches who were believed to do evil (by putting curses on people and so forth), but also the ones who healed the sick. Their work was not considered medicine, but magic—and church leaders believed entirely in the power of magic. Furthermore, they were afraid of it, in large part because it gave the poorer, peasant classes independence from its authority.

The famous European witch hunts went on for some 400 years, and somewhere between a few hundred thousand people and several million people were tortured and executed for the crime of witchcraft. The majority of them were women. It's not possible to know how many of these people were accused of witchcraft because of their use of magic-medicine or for some other reason entirely, but Christianity's perception of witches has shaped our often shady view of them ever since. Traditional healing methods were further marginalized in Europe during the thirteenth century, when medicine was established as a profession—which, of course, excluded women.

We're not suggesting that these practices and beliefs have been handed down in one continuous, unbroken line, but we can point to certain historical moments that inform our present-day, plant-based healing traditions. Here in the Americas we draw from a number of different traditions, and people often practice a combination of a few (whether they realize it or not). In the U.S. South in particular, so-called folk magic is a blend of African, European, and Indigenous traditions. In the Appalachian region, Cherokee and Choctaw people shared their knowledge with white settlers, mostly Scots-Irish and English, who'd brought their own beliefs about plant healing from their home countries. The earliest Black Americans also learned the use of

Plant Magic

For thousands of years, people around the world have attributed magical and spiritual powers to herb plants. Even if you're not interested in working with plants to cast spells, this is a rich and fascinating subject. Many books have been written about herbal magic, and even practical-minded gardening books often address plants' spiritual uses. Herbal knowledge is often intertwined with herbal lore, like a vine with many tendrils.

In the late 19th century, an Englishman named Richard Folkard compiled a huge compendium of plant lore, which he'd gathered over the years that he worked for a horticulture journal. Here are a few tidbits from his book, which is available to read online for free and is long-windedly titled *Plant Lore, Legends, and Lyrics: Embracing the Myths, Traditions, Superstitions, and Folk-lore of the Plant Kingdom.*

- The herb vervain was sacred to people around the world, including the Druids, who used it for divination, and the ancient Egyptians, who believed it grew from the tears cried by the goddess Isis.

- English witches believed that catnip would make even the calmest person angry and argumentative.

- Mistletoe hung in the windows of a house could protect the people inside it from evil spirits and curses.

- Rosemary, if worn on the body, has been said to improve a person's memory. There is also a Sicilian legend that calls rosemary the fairies' favorite plant, and says that they can be found hiding under it in the form of snakes.

- In the South and West of England, a young woman could dream of her future husband by picking a yarrow plant that she found growing on a young man's grave and then sleeping with it under her pillow.

native plants from Indigenous people, and they practiced herb doctoring in West African and Caribbean traditions. In her book *African American Folk Healing*, Stephanie Mitchem writes that during the times of enslavement and segregation, white doctors would not treat Black patients, so they had to rely on their own knowledge. Furthermore, doctors of the white medical establishment frequently sought the advice of enslaved women practitioners, which they then shared with the formal medical community. Further south, the Aztecs had hundreds upon hundreds of plant remedies for health, healing, and beauty—so many, in fact, that the Spanish *conquistadors*, who had relatively little of this type of knowledge, were astounded. Today people of Mexican descent use many of these plants in the same ways their ancestors did.

Throughout history, the use of plants to heal and protect has never gone away—it just goes underground. Knowing that by putting these ideas into practice we're participating in ancient traditions makes us feel good. It also makes us feel *witchy*: wise and knowledgeable, connected to nature and to the people in our communities who have shared their knowledge with us, including the many who lived and died long before we came along.

What Makes This Relevant Today?

We are living in a moment of renewed interest in the mystical. Call it New Age or 'Woo,' call it Witchcraft or the Intuitive Arts or Mind-Body-Spirit; name yourself Bruja or Conjure or Pagan or Priest/ess. ... It makes sense to me. Our future-focused, technology-obsessed world seems to be hurtling down a bad path. People are turning to ancestral practices for a sense of enduring longevity, and comfort. ... To source a different kind of power in hopes of making changes both personal and political.

–Michelle Tea, *Modern Tarot*

We're sure you've seen it: Witchy imagery is everywhere. Spooky fashion has gone mainstream, the internet is exploding with natural DIYs, and it's never been easier to buy a deck of tarot cards. It seems that lots of people are being drawn to nature-based practices for the first time, while other more experienced folks are finding the cultural climate safe enough for them to come out of the broom closet. We think there are some very valid reasons for this recent trend.

Life on this planet is endangered, and many of us feel called to do something about it. We want—need—to nurture a connection to the Earth.

And as it happens, the products we use every day can have an impact on our health, as well as on the health of our planet. While we as individuals can't solve the environmental crisis, we can take control over the products we bring into our homes. Using cleaning and personal care products exposes us—and our children and pets—to a range of chemicals, both synthetic and of natural origin. Some of these chemicals can cause allergic reactions, and some contaminate our waterways after they get washed down the drain. In the United States, most products do not have to be proven safe before they are put on the market, which leaves consumers potentially vulnerable. Even less consideration is taken for a product's environmental impact.

In her 2017 book *The Case Against Fragrance*, writer Kate Grenville looks at how many commercial products used to clean the home or beautify the body are made and the effects they can have on us. Her findings are undeniably distressing. She cites a 2014 U.S. study that showed that, of the migraine patients whose headaches were caused by smells, "perfume" was a trigger for almost three quarters of them. Canadian researchers also recently found evidence that, in some cases, asthma is primarily aggravated by artificial scents. Even when synthetic fragrances, often made from petrochemicals, are chemically identical to their natural counterparts, they can cause allergic reactions when added in unnaturally large quantities.

Unfortunately, it is often impossible to avoid the triggering ingredients by reading package labels, since many of them aren't listed. Scent blends are considered trade secrets, which means manufacturers aren't required to disclose their ingredients. A label of "fragrance" or "perfume" is good enough—and a typical fragrance might contain a hundred or more chemicals. This lack of transparency makes it difficult, if not impossible, for consumers to know what exactly they're buying.

The existence of these kinds of loopholes means that there could be some real nasties lurking in your kitchen cabinet or makeup bag. This makes us mad. It also makes us want to take action. When you can't trust that the products on the shelves are safe, making your own—often using simple and old-fashioned methods—is an act of empowerment. Marketers may have taken the language of self-care and perverted it, telling us we're being kind to ourselves by buying more and more, but we believe that true self-care means gaining the knowledge you need to protect yourself and the environment. That way, you can take matters into your own hands.

Creating Community

One of the most exciting things about kitchen witchery is that it's an excellent basis for community building. The knowledge of natural living is inherently communal after all. Sharing what you know and learning from other people can be a joyous, lifelong process.

As you read this book you'll see that, in addition to being written by two friends, it has a whole chorus of voices behind it. Parents and grandparents, neighborhood gardeners, local herbalists, the public library—ideas in natural living come from, and are routinely shared with, a whole network of people. Resources like these are most likely available to you too.

As you continue to get excited about natural living, you might like to create these kinds of community connections yourself. Children can be your helpers in the kitchen and garden from a young age, and they love to make crafts. How beautiful would it be to give them a hands-on lesson in environmentalism at the kitchen table?

You could also consider donating the goods you make, giving them as gifts, or even trading them. A friend of ours who grew up in a rural area told us that, when she was a child, her parents would plan their large garden based on what their neighbors were growing. As they harvested their beans, they'd trade some for a neighbor's eggplant or tomatoes. Think about asking if your neighbors or friends are into trading homegrown or homemade products with you.

Skill-sharing workshops are another wonderful way to connect with like-minded people, and they don't have to be in any way formal. You could simply invite a few people over to your kitchen to show them how to do something you've learned from this book. Maybe you already know how to knit, and you want to learn how to bind a book by hand. Find someone who's interested in learning what you know and swap lessons.

If you don't have space at home for a garden of your own, there's very likely a community garden near you. You might be amazed by how much you can grow on a tiny plot in a shared space. Likewise, there are community garden clubs throughout the country. Check the website of the National Garden Clubs, Inc. to see if there's one local to you. We have gained a ton of knowledge by attending the free and inexpensive workshops and talks hosted by groups like these, and their older members are a fount of information.

Above all, remember this: You create community just by participating in it. So go ahead and dive in!

The Well-Stocked Cupboard

Just like keeping a good selection of pantry staples on hand allows you to create a variety of dishes with just a few core ingredients, a well-stocked cupboard will do the same for your household and personal care recipes. You may already have a few of these ingredients in your kitchen, and most can be picked up at the grocery store. Some of the more specialty ingredients could require a visit to a natural food store, apothecary, herb shop, or online retailer. Our recommended sources for ingredients can be found in the *Resources* section.

We strongly suggest keeping a dedicated set of pots, bowls, measuring cups, and so on separate from the ones you use for cooking and baking. This greatly reduces the chance of non-edible ingredients accidentally coming into contact with food. You can often find inexpensive and perfectly serviceable kitchen equipment at thrift stores, so this extra set doesn't have to cost much.

Equipment

Bucket You'll need at least one of these. A typical household bucket holds 3 gallons of liquid, which is plenty big enough to clean your bathroom or kitchen. Get a sturdy one with thick walls.

Cheesecloth Traditionally used in cheesemaking, this cotton cloth can be used to strain plant fibers and other small solids that might fall through a mesh strainer.

Cotton cloths/rags We prefer these to paper products that create unnecessary waste and don't even hold up very well when used for cleaning. Consider buying some 100% cotton cloths (i.e., washcloths, diapers), tearing up worn out clothing and towels, or knitting your own.

Double boiler This is just what it sounds like: two pots, one on top of the other. It is used when heating or melting something on the stove that shouldn't sit too close to the heat source. You can purchase a double boiler or a double boiler insert to fit over a pot you already own, or see the *Techniques* section for instructions on how to improvise one.

Funnel This useful tool, which is available in a variety of sizes, will come in handy when you need to pour liquids or small solids into a container with a small mouth.

Glass containers Canning jars are excellent for storing your homemade concoctions. So are cleaned up jars that hold store-bought food. Preparations that need protection from sunlight can be stored in bottles and jars made of dark blue or amber glass. Different kinds of dispensers are available for bottles, such as droppers, spray nozzles, and pumps.

Gloves When working with ingredients like borax and washing soda, or with the finished cleaning products you've made, wear rubber gloves to avoid skin irritation.

Labels Be sure to label every jar, bottle, and tin you fill with your homemade concoctions so you don't confuse them. Include the date you make each product, since you'll want to use it before it loses its potency or expires. A paper label with an adhesive back does the trick.

Measuring cups and spoons You probably already have a set of these, but we recommend getting an extra one to use just for kitchen witch projects.

Medicine measuring cup Unlike a kitchen measuring cup, this has fluid ounces and milliliters marked on it, which makes it invaluable for measuring out liquids in very small quantities. You can buy one of these at the pharmacy or save one that comes with a bottle of medicine.

Mortar and pestle Historically used by apothecaries and still a symbol of pharmacies today, this ancient stone tool crushes herbs into powder with ease.

Muslin drawstring bags These little cotton bags can be used to brew tea, to add herbs to a bath, and for quick, no-sew sachets to freshen stale-smelling drawers. They can be washed and reused over and over.

Pots Set aside a dedicated pot or two for heating up ingredients to make household cleaners on the stovetop. Don't use these for cooking food.

Strainer This is an indispensable tool for making tinctures, infusions, and decoctions, all of which require liquid to be separated from plant matter. It needs to be made of a fine mesh to do its job well, but depending on the plant material, sometimes a cheesecloth will work better.

Teapot It's nice to have a proper teapot for preparing hot water infusions. The spout makes it easy to neatly pour out the liquid.

Tin containers Metal tins, available in a range of sizes, make great containers for balms.

Wooden spoon As with the cooking pots, set aside a wooden spoon for stirring household cleaners, particularly those that need to be made over heat on the stovetop, and don't use it for cooking or baking food.

Ingredients

Aloe vera This succulent is a common houseplant whose leaves produce a clear gel that has been used to soothe sunburns and wounds, among other uses, for centuries. Keep one (or more) in your home and you'll always have some first-aid ointment on hand. Alternatively, you can buy aloe vera gel, with minimal added ingredients, and use it for skincare applications.

Apple cider vinegar (ACV) Made from fermented apples, ACV contains acetic acid just like distilled white vinegar, as well as malic acid. It comes in two varieties: filtered and raw (unfiltered). Filtered works best for cleaning and for hair rinses. The raw, unfiltered kind contains bacteria that some people believe provide health benefits when taken internally. Just in case these bacteria are good for your skin too, use the raw variety in skincare.

Arrowroot powder Soft and absorbent, it is used in recipes for body powders and deodorants. Cornstarch does the same thing.

Baking soda This chemical compound (sodium bicarbonate) can do many jobs around the house besides baking. It neutralizes odors and gently scrubs all kinds of surfaces in the kitchen and bathroom, among other uses.

Beeswax This old-fashioned ingredient can be used in the home and on the body. It is sold in blocks that can be chopped up or grated and can be found as small pellets called pastilles. Carnauba wax is a vegan alternative for skincare applications.

Borax Also known as sodium borate, borax is a mineral that kills mold and mildew, making it an excellent bathroom cleaner. Keep it stored safely away from small children and animals, as it is toxic if ingested. We use the "20 Mule Team" kind in a box. (Fun fact: The 20 Mule Team trademarked name refers to the way the mineral was excavated from Death Valley after large quantities of it were discovered there in the 1880s.)

Butter Shea butter and cocoa butter are common skincare ingredients. They add moisturizing properties to homemade balms and they each can be used alone as a simple moisturizer. Shea butter is available in two varieties: refined and unrefined. Cocoa butter is available in three forms: in a container, as a chunk or block, or as small wafers.

Castile soap Named after Castile, Spain, a city once famous for producing soap made from olive oil, castile soap today (available in liquid and bar form) is made up of a variety of plant oils. It is biodegradable and therefore quite safe for the environment, and can be used on the body and all over the house. We like the soap from Dr. Bronner's, a brand that was started in the 1940s, because it contains minimal ingredients. You can add your own essential oils to their unscented liquid soap, or choose a soap that is already scented with essential oils like lavender, peppermint, tea tree, eucalyptus, or a citrus blend.

Citric acid Naturally occurring in citrus fruits, citric acid is added to many foods to preserve or flavor them. Because it is a (weak) acid, it is also very useful for cleaning. Be sure to buy pure citric acid, not the kind mixed with an anti-caking agent.

Clay, cosmetic Their exact properties vary, but each kind of clay— bentonite, kaolin (a.k.a. white or china), French green, pink, rhassoul—draws out impurities from the skin and absorbs moisture.

Distilled water Distilled water does not contain minerals and other impurities that could be present in tap water (even when filtered), which then end up in your water-based recipes. Minerals can build up in containers and clog pumps and spray nozzles. Old recipes sometimes call for springwater or rainwater out of concern for water purity; distilled water makes a good substitute. Find it in the bottled water section of the grocery store or make it at home following the instructions provided in *Techniques*.

Distilled white vinegar This inexpensive household staple uses the power of acetic acid to clean almost anything. Go ahead and get the big bottle because you'll never want to be without it. It deodorizes, cuts through oil and grease, and has been proven to be as effective as bleach at eliminating E. coli from surfaces. When making cleaning solutions, you might use the vinegar straight, diluted with water, or infused with herbs. For details on making an herb-infused vinegar, see *Techniques*.

Essential oils (EOs) Also called the essence of a plant, these extracts are valued for their fragrance and antimicrobial properties. See *Essential Oils, Hydrosols, and Aromatherapy* for more information.

Grain alcohol This is commonly sold in concentrations of 120, 151, and 190 proof (60%, 75.5%, and 95% alcohol respectively). We use it to solubilize, or dissolve, essential oils so that they can be used safely in water or water-based mixtures. A higher concentration of alcohol is better for this purpose.

Herbs The witchiest ingredient in the cupboard, herbs of all kinds are used in many applications for the home and body. Grow them yourself, buy them fresh from the grocery store or dried from the herb shop, or check your herbal tea collection or spice rack for something suitable when in need.

Honey, raw A traditional remedy to heal wounds, raw (unpasteurized) honey's humectant and antibacterial properties make it a skincare ingredient that can benefit all skin types.

Hydrosols When essential oils are created using steam distillation, the water that separates from the oil is called a hydrosol. See *Essential Oils, Hydrosols, and Aromatherapy* for more information.

Lemon juice The citric acid in lemons makes it useful for cleaning. It can brighten white laundry and clean tarnish off of copper, among other things. Squeeze it straight from the lemon, or keep a store-bought bottle of pure lemon juice in the fridge to have on hand any time you need it.

Oats Colloidal oatmeal (finely ground up whole oats) is the active ingredient in many skincare products formulated to soothe dry, itchy skin. Homemade preparations of rolled oats provide similar benefits.

Oils Both culinary (i.e., cooking) and skincare oils can be used on skin and hair. Culinary oils (extra virgin olive, avocado, raw and unrefined coconut, etc.) work best for rinse-off recipes and in rich balms, while skincare oils (sweet almond, jojoba, rosehip seed, etc.) are better suited for leave-on applications. Culinary oils should be cold-pressed and, when applicable, raw and unrefined, to ensure that they are pure and retain as much of their natural properties as possible.

Pine rosin This is a solid resin produced by pine trees. It comes in the form of small pebble-like pieces that melt when heated. We use a refined rosin to make food wraps for the kitchen.

Rubbing alcohol Also known by its scientific name, isopropyl alcohol, this first-aid remedy is commonly used to clean wounds because it kills bacteria. It also helps around the house by disinfecting surfaces, cutting through oil, and removing stubborn sticky substances. We recommend 70% for everyday use.

Salt People have been using salt to soothe and heal skin for thousands of years. Unrefined salts like Himalyan salt, sea salt, and Dead Sea salt contain minerals that may provide skincare benefits. While most salts are made of sodium chloride, Epsom salt, named after a town in England where it was abundant, is made of magnesium sulfate. Though it has many uses, it is probably best known as a bath salt. Today commercial Epsom salt is created synthetically.

Sugar Its gritty texture and glycolic acid make sugar an effective physical and chemical skin exfoliator.

Vegetable glycerine Often called glycerin on product labels, this thick, clear liquid is commonly used in skincare products for its moisturizing properties.

Washing soda Washing soda is a chemical compound that comes in a white powder form. Commercially, both washing soda and borax are called "detergent boosters," and they can be used together or separately in homemade laundry soaps and other household cleaners.

Witch hazel This is a distilled extract made from the bark of the witch hazel tree (*Hamamelis virginiana*). When mixed in a product with alcohol it's called an astringent, which is used to clean and help heal minor cuts, burns, and bruises. Witch hazel toner is a skincare product that deep-cleans and balances skin.

Essential Oils, Hydrosols, and Aromatherapy

The world of essential oils is so complex it requires its own section. Here we will go over important details about essential oils, including safety precautions, that you need to know before using them in recipes. Also included is information about hydrosols, what they are and how to use them. Finally, we provide a brief description of aromatherapy, which is the practice of using scents for wellbeing.

The Essentials of Essential Oil

An essential oil is a fragrant liquid extracted from plants. It contains the so-called *essence* or *spirit* of the plant, which is composed of a multitude of chemicals. Various plant parts, such as leaves, flowers, fruit peels, seeds, roots, and even some tree resins are used to make essential oils. There are several methods by which essential oils are obtained, such as expression (pressing the plant material, like citrus fruit rind) and steam distillation.

For thousands of years humans have used plants for their fragrance and medicinal properties. While ancient people did not understand exactly how certain plants could heal, presumably their treatments worked well enough, at least some of the time. Our ancestors did not always distinguish between ailments of the body and the mind, and they sometimes attributed disease to supernatural causes. In a world where body, mind, and spirit are not considered separate entities, it might be believed that a particular essential oil literally wards off evil spirits while in reality it is the scent of the oil that triggers feelings of calm and wellbeing, thus banishing a bad mood.

Today, aromatherapists, in the tradition of the medieval apothecary, prescribe oils to soothe and heal the body, mind, and spirit. Scientists study their chemicals seeking potential medicinal and industrial applications. Many common, commercially produced household and personal care products contain essential oils. Likewise, we use essential oils to give our homemade products beautiful aromas, as antimicrobials, and for their potentially beneficial skincare properties. While essential oils are not technically essential to a kitchen witch's cupboard, these potions do add a lot of charm to any recipe they're in.

Shopping for Essential Oils

Unfortunately, there is no oversight body that regulates the production and sale of essential oils, so you just have to trust that the bottle actually contains what is stated on the label. Because certain essential oils are so expensive to produce, companies could be tempted to pass off adulterated or synthetic oils as the real thing. For this reason we buy only from established companies whose products tend to be sold in natural food stores and in specialty shops like apothecaries that also sell natural ingredients for DIY products. We assume these stores have high standards for the quality of products they sell. We also look at the company's website to see whether they explain how they source their ingredients and if they take the issue of sustainability seriously.

Safety Precautions

Although something described as a plant's spirit may seem like a harmless thing, essential oils are highly concentrated chemicals and should be treated with the same respect as anything found in a chemistry lab. Always read the label carefully and follow its instructions. Store essential oils in a cool, dark, and dry place. They can last for a few years, but they will deteriorate over time, making them potentially unsafe to use on skin. Use only newer oils for skincare and reserve the older ones for household use and aromatherapy. They can also be flammable, so keep them away from high heat and open flames, and take care when using them in diffusers with candles.

Before working with essential oils, consult your healthcare provider if you are taking any medication, have a known or suspected medical condition, are pregnant or nursing, or have any known or suspected allergies to the plant from which an essential oil was extracted. It is recommended that all essential oils be used only very moderately during the first trimester of pregnancy and some should be avoided entirely. Never use essential oils internally. Don't use them on or around children or pets. Be cautious about using them anywhere near cats in particular, as they can cause extreme irritation to the respiratory tract and can lead to other health problems.

While certain essential oils can be used neat (i.e., directly on the skin), most need to be mixed with a carrier oil—any culinary or skincare oil—or within a product that contains oil, like a balm, in order to be used on skin safely. Some companies sell bottles of essential oil mixed with a carrier oil. The labels on these bottles state something like "[essential oil] in [carrier] oil." This allows companies to offer very expensive essential oils at a more affordable price and makes the essential oil ready to use on skin. These pre-mixed oils should only be used in recipes that call for an oil or a butter, and they should not be placed in diffusers or used with steam or in water-based recipes. For example, you wouldn't want to spray a cleaning solution containing jojoba oil onto a countertop since it would only make a bigger mess!

It's a good idea to read up on every essential oil before using it, or better yet, before even making a purchase. Each kind of essential oil has unique properties. For example, certain citrus-derived essential oils contain chemicals called furanocoumarins that can cause a skin reaction known as photosensitivity. So, when sunlight shines on skin that is covered with an essential oil containing furanocoumarins, the resulting chemical reaction can damage skin cells. As we've said, essential oils are powerful chemicals and must be handled with great care. We strongly encourage you to read books and articles written by experts before experimenting with essential oils. See our recommendations at the end of this book.

Hydrosols

We can't talk about essential oils without also mentioning hydrosols, sometimes referred to as hydrolats. These fragrant waters are created by the same steam distillation process that produces essential oils. They contain some of the chemicals found in essential oils, but in a much less concentrated form. It is believed that hydrosols provide skincare benefits, just like certain essential oils. Yet unlike most essential oils, they can be applied directly to the skin. Hydrosols have a strong fragrance, and can be used purely for aromatherapeutic purposes. They should be stored in a cool, dry, and dark place. When the liquid in the bottle begins to look cloudy, it's time to throw it out.

If you read a lot of skincare labels, you have probably come across the term "flower water" or "[name of flower] water." This may or may not refer to a hydrosol. Because hydrosols, like essential oils, are not regulated in any way, there is no standard naming or labeling protocol to which companies must adhere. Some flower waters are actually decoctions, which are made by placing plant material, like rose petals, in water, bringing it to a boil, and then straining the plant material away. This decoction or flower water could contain some beneficial properties and it would certainly smell like the plant material, but it would probably not contain all the same kinds of chemical compounds that would be present in a hydrosol made from the same plant. Another kind of flower water is made from essential oils that have been added to water. Even if the essential oils have been properly solubilized, this is still not a hydrosol.

Whether any of these distinctions matter depends on your needs. All of these plant-derived waters will have a scent, which may be all you need from them, and so how they got their scent is irrelevant. But for purists and anyone who really takes the whole "spirit of the plant" idea seriously, true hydrosols contain a bit of that essence from the essential oils, which was removed from the plant at the same time the hydrosol was created. So, if an essential oil really does help with a particular skin condition, then the hydrosol could, too. And if you believe that essential oils offer some sort of metaphysical benefits because they allow you to work with a plant's energy, then hydrosols would also contain a bit of that spirit.

Building an Essential Oil Collection

When first dipping into the world of essential oils you may feel compelled to buy a bunch of them just because they could be useful at some point. We do not advise doing this. Just focus on the basics, or the ones you feel drawn to. Once you get the hang of essential oils, a collection that suits your needs will come about naturally.

Below is a list of all of the essential oils mentioned in this book along with some of their properties and safety precautions.Never use essential oils on or around children or animals. Take extra care when working with the following in a home with pets, as they can be particularly poisonous to dogs and cats if ingested or applied directly to the skin: bergamot, eucalyptus, grapefruit, lemon, orange, peppermint, pine, and tea tree.

Atlas cedarwood (*Cedrus atlantica*). A sweet, woody scent commonly associated with cedar chests and closets that is believed to repel moths. Antiseptic.

Bergamot (*Citrus bergamia*). A citrusy scent common in perfumery, and the starring flavor of Earl Grey tea. It is available in "bergaptene-free" form (bergaptene is a kind of furocoumarin, the chemicals that cause photosensitivity when used on skin). Antibacterial.

Citronella (*Cymbopogon winterianus*). A strong, citrusy scent that is frequently used in candles and other products meant to repel mosquitoes. Antibacterial, antifungal. Avoid applying to skin during pregnancy.

Eucalyptus (*Eucalyptus globulus* or *Eucalyptus radiata*). A strong, menthol-like scent commonly associated with decongestants. Antibacterial.

Fir, silver (*Abies alba*). An evergreen with a fresh but almost sweet scent. Antiseptic. Avoid if you have respiratory issues.

Frankincense (*Boswellia sacra, Boswellia carteri*, and others*). A resin extract from tree bark, it has a deep, spicy, woody scent. Used as a sacred fragrance by different religions since ancient times, it was one of the gifts of the Biblical Three Wisemen, and so it's often associated with Christmas. Antibacterial.

Grapefruit (*Citrus paradisi*). A bitter citrus scent that stimulates the mind and helps with concentration. Antiseptic. Photosensitizing.

Juniper berry (*Juniperus communis*). Smells bracing, like a walk in the woods. Juniper berries are the star ingredient in gin. Antiseptic. Avoid during pregnancy or if you have kidney or liver disease.

Lavender (*Lavandula angustifolia* or *lavandula officinalis*). The lavender plant is named after the Latin word for washing, *lavare*, because the Ancient Romans used it in their baths. The scent is relaxing, and commonly used to promote sleep. Antibacterial, antifungal.

Lemon (*Citrus limon*). The ultimate uplifting citrus scent, makes everything smell clean and sparkling. Antimicrobial. Photosensitizing.

Orange, sweet (*Citrus sinensis*). Smells bright and clean like lemon, but warmer. Mood lifting. Antibacterial.

Patchouli (*Pogostemon cablin*). The classic hippie scent, it's earthy, grounding, and calming. Works well as a deodorizer on bodies and in the air. Antimicrobial.

Peppermint (*Mentha piperita*). Perhaps the most popular of all the mints. Detested by mice and many insects. Can energize or calm as needed (i.e., it is an adaptogen). Antibacterial. Avoid during pregnancy.

Rosemary (*Rosmarinus officinalis*). A bright scent reminiscent of mint, but spicier. Disliked by many household "pests." Antimicrobial. Avoid during pregnancy.

Tea tree (*Melaleuca alternifolia*). A distinct, almost medicinal scent. Commonly used in skincare to combat acne and may be found in the first-aid aisle of pharmacies. Antibacterial, antiviral, antifungal.

Thyme, white (*Thymus vulgaris* or *thymus zygis*). Smells medicinal, a bit like eucalyptus. Antibacterial, antiviral, antifungal. Avoid during pregnancy.

Aromatherapy

In making their gardens and choosing their flowers, the ancients had a profound feeling for the lovely quality of fragrance.

–Henry Beston, *Herbs and the Earth*

Of the five senses, our sense of smell is perhaps the most enigmatic. We use it constantly but generally notice it only when our noses detect something jarring. Odors tell us if food has spoiled, alert us to the presence of a nearby fire, and they can transport us through time and space when we smell a scent that evokes a strong memory. Scent is deeply associated with enhancing both memory and taste. Olfactory sensors provide a direct connection between the external world and our minds, where scents affect us on both the conscious and subconscious levels.

Because we know all this about our sense of smell we can use scents in a deliberate way to alter our moods and enhance our wellbeing. This is called aromatherapy. While synthetic scents do have an impact on us, there is something special about the highly concentrated fragrance that comes directly from a plant, i.e., an essential oil, and so that is what aromatherapists work with in their practice. Of course, anyone can buy essential oils and use them in their personal care routines and around their home, though it is advisable to consult books and articles written by professionals before experimenting.

Putting essential oil aromas to work for you can be done via several methods. The simplest is just to keep a bottle of essential oil close by and take a sniff whenever you need it. If that's not practical, place a few drops on a tissue and carry it around in your sleeve or pocket. Any personal care product—balm, body oil, castile soap, and so on—that has essential oils in it will provide aromatherapeutic benefits when you use that product. Room sprays, cleaning solutions, candles, wax melts, and essential oil diffusers can all distribute beneficial scents around a home.

Preparation, Clean-up, and Storage

Though it may seem fussy, preparing your workspace, cleaning up well, and storing your products properly are all important parts of the DIY process. Using the right tools in the right way ensures your safety and will help make the recipes come out right.

Preparation of Containers

Thoroughly wash containers and lids and make sure they have completely dried before using them. Containers for skincare products should also be disinfected. Pour a bit of rubbing (isopropyl) alcohol (70% or higher) inside the container, close the lid, and then slowly turn the container over and over, making sure the alcohol touches all parts of the interior. Let that sit for a few minutes with the lid on to allow the alcohol to kill any germs. Alcohol will also help remove any oily residue. Open the lid, pour out the alcohol, and let the container air dry.

Alternatively, if you want to use proper canning jars as containers, you can place them into boiling water just as you would to sterilize them for canning food. Consult a reputable canning source for detailed instructions.

Cleaning Up

Using a separate set of equipment (pots, bowls, spoons, etc.) from the ones reserved for cooking and baking not only ensures that you won't accidentally ingest something non-edible, but it also makes clean-up much more efficient since you don't have to worry too much about getting things *perfectly* clean.

Wash your cotton cleaning rags after every use. This is especially important when you've cleaned something grimy, like the kitchen floor or anything in the bathroom. Get them in the washer right away, along with laundry soap and hot water.

The most stubborn substance to clean up is beeswax. The following tips should address most situations you'll encounter when working with this tricky ingredient.

- For a thick layer stuck to a container (like a bowl or jar) put the container into the freezer and leave it for at least an hour. Once frozen, the wax should pop out with minimal effort.

- For a thin coating inside a container (like a bowl or pot), heat up the container and then wipe away the warm wax with a rag. Throw the rag away. Never pour wax down the drain as it can clog the pipes.

- To clean up the residue left behind in an otherwise clean container, sprinkle on some baking soda and scrub the surface with a damp sponge. Then wash with dish soap. Baking soda will also remove residue from your hands.

- For spills on countertops, let the beeswax cool and harden, and then scrape it off. If a residue remains, sprinkle on some baking soda. Using a damp sponge, scrub off the residue, and then wipe the spot clean with your usual countertop cleaner.

- For beeswax that's combined with oils and/or butters inside a container, heat up the container and wipe out as much as you can with a rag. Throw the rag away. To remove the remaining residue, mix up a paste of baking soda and dish soap on a different surface, like a plate or the countertop. Dab a damp sponge or rag into the paste and then use that to scrub off the residue. Rinse the container with hot water.

Storage and Shelf Life

You do not need a huge house with lots of storage space to be a good kitchen witch. A cabinet, dresser, or shelf that stays cool and dry throughout the year will work well for most things, and the fridge will temporarily preserve those that spoil more quickly. The recipes in this book are meant to be made in small batches and used sooner rather than later, in large part because they don't contain preservatives like commercial products do. Consider putting away only what you think you'll use soon and giving away the rest; a jar of homemade laundry soap, for example, would make a lovely and unique housewarming gift.

Storing Dry Products

Store dry ingredients in "non-reactive" containers, such as ones made of stainless steel, ceramic, glass, or plastic.

Store dried herbs in glass jars. Dark glass will keep them protected from sunlight, but clear glass jars kept in a dark cabinet, kitchen cupboard, or even a dresser, will work just fine. (For more on harvesting and storing herbs, see pages 108-119.) Stored properly, most dried herbs will be useful for at least a year.

Storing Liquid Products

Store essential oils in a cool, dark, and dry place. Their shelf life ranges from about one to four years. Because an older essential oil may have a slightly different chemical makeup than a newer one, use only newer essential oils in skincare to reduce the risk of irritation.

Water-based products like infusions and decoctions should be stored in the fridge. Some last a few days, others a few months, depending on what is mixed with the water. If a misty cloud has developed in the liquid, the product has spoiled and should be thrown away.

Most alcohol-based tinctures should last for a few years. Store them away from direct sunlight.

Vinegar infusions have a shelf life of around six months. Store them in a glass jar using a lid that is not made of metal, as the vinegar will corrode it.

Balms should be stored in metal tins or glass jars away from heat. Let your nose tell you when a balm has turned. However, for balms that are applied to skin, it's probably best to toss them after six months even if they still smell fine. The inclusion of beeswax may help inhibit the growth of microbes, and antimicrobial essential oils may also help extend a balm's shelf life. Vitamin E and rosemary extract are two antioxidants that can be added to balms to help preserve them.

Skincare oils should be stored in a cool, dry, and dark place, though some, like rosehip seed oil, need to be refrigerated. Follow the instructions on the label.

Techniques and Conversions

I n order to use plant matter or plant essence in your DIY body care and household products, you'll need to know a few techniques. The following is a guide to the ones we refer to throughout the book. Check here for detailed instructions, as well as the measurement conversions you'll use most often.

Double Boiler

A double boiler is a pair of two pots, one on top of the other, also called a *bain-marie*. Water is boiled in the bottom pot while the vessel on top holds something solid, like chocolate or beeswax, that needs to be melted gently, away from the direct heat of the stove. You can buy a proper double boiler or make your own using two pots, one slightly smaller than the other, or a pot and a heatproof bowl that fits on top of the pot.

Alternatively, a heatproof vessel like a canning jar or a bowl or cup made of Pyrex glass set into an inch or two of water also works well. Try using the screw-on lid that goes with the canning jar as a platform for the jar to sit on—that way, the jar will be set above the bottom of the pot and the water. Its contents will get heated up and melted by the steam.

Solubilization

There are a great many homemade air freshener recipes out there, in blogs and major magazines alike, that tell you to simply add essential oils to water or witch hazel in a spray bottle. Unfortunately, this doesn't work as well as it could. Essential oils, like any oil, can't really dissolve in either water or witch hazel, which is water-based. If you were to do it this way the oils would remain separate from the rest of the solution, which isn't totally effective or safe—especially if the oils in the spray could be damaging to your skin or a household surface. Shaking the solution before you use the spray will temporarily break down the oils, but there's a better method. Let's look to the experts for help.

The Tisserand Institute, which provides educational resources on the safe use of essential oils, recommends using grain alcohol to solubilize—that is, dissolve—any essential oils that you add to household sprays like room fresheners. Tisserand advises that a room spray be made up of at least 20 percent grain alcohol that is at least 151 proof. We like to make it 25 percent, and use 151-proof grain alcohol. Putting the essential oils in the grain alcohol in the right proportions and letting the solution sit for at least a few hours will ensure that the oils have broken down, at which point you can add the whole thing to water. The grain alcohol also helps inhibit the growth of microbes (you know, germs) in your solution.

Infusions, Tinctures, and Decoctions

Infusions, tinctures, and decoctions are liquids that have absorbed the properties of a plant, including its scent. Herbal infusions are made by steeping herbs in a liquid. Tinctures are stronger and more concentrated than infusions, and they're made by steeping herb plants in alcohol. Decoctions use boiling water to break down the plant material. All of these have a number of different uses.

Infusions

Infusions are liquids that have had plant matter infused in them, so that the plant's properties are extracted into the liquid. For instance, every time you brew tea, using either the leaf of the tea plant or an herb for herbal tea, you are making a hot water infusion.

Hot water infusion

Dried plant matter

Water, boiled

Teapot

Place one to two teaspoons of the dried plant matter into a teapot and add in one cup of boiling water. Let it steep for at least five minutes. The precise measurements and steep times vary depending on the plant and the desired strength of the infusion.

Other liquids can be infused with herbs too, including honey, oil, and vinegar. These all have different properties and uses, and they can be made with or without heating. Herb-infused oils can be used as body oils, and both infused oil and vinegar make delicious additions to a salad or other recipe. An herb-infused vinegar is also very handy around the house. For cleaning jobs that call for vinegar, using one that's been infused with herbs will give it a nice scent and antimicrobial properties.

Vinegar infusion

Herb cuttings, fresh or dried

Distilled white vinegar

Container with a lid that's not made of metal

Label

To make an herb-infused vinegar, you can either cut a few sprigs from a living plant or work with plants that have already been dried. The experienced folks at Mountain Rose Herbs recommend this simple rule of measurement, which works well: Use twice as much vinegar as herbs when working with fresh-cut ones, and 15 times as much for dried herbs.

Put the plant matter in an empty container, then pour distilled white vinegar over it, making sure to cover the plants completely. Neither the container nor the lid can be made of metal, as the vinegar will corrode it. Parchment paper held on with rubber bands will perfectly cover a glass canning jar. Be sure to label your infusion with its contents and the date—once you've made more than one of these it's easy to get confused. Then put it in a cool, dark place. This technique doesn't need total darkness to work, just don't leave your container in direct sunlight.

After one to four weeks, strain the plants out using cheesecloth or a fine strainer. Discard or compost the plant material and start putting your infused vinegar to work in any cleaning recipe that calls for vinegar.

Oil infusion
Herbs, dried
Skincare oil
Glass jar
Label

To make an herb-infused oil to use on the face or body, place the herbs into a glass jar, then fill the jar, not quite to the top, with oil. Or, if making an infusion with a pigmented herb, such as alkanet root, use only enough oil to cover the herb so that the oil gets as much color as possible. Shake the jar to mix the herbs and oil together, and then set it aside, away from sunlight. But first, put a label on the jar with the date so that you can keep track of when you made it. Shake the jar every day for at least two weeks. Then strain the oil through a fine mesh strainer or cheesecloth into another jar. Store this infused oil away from heat and light. If it starts to look or smell odd, throw it away.

An alternative method comes from a blog post on the Mountain Rose Herbs website, which states that instead of keeping the jar in the dark during the infusion process, you can set it in a warm, sunny spot to allow the sun to help the herbs and oil blend together. This is probably not advisable for oil that you're trying to dye, since sunlight may alter the color.

Tinctures

Tinctures are stronger and more concentrated than infusions. They are made by steeping plant matter, either fresh-cut or dried, in alcohol or a mixture of alcohol and water. The most common alcohols to use for this purpose are vodka and grain alcohol, but other spirits, such as brandy, will also work. We prefer grain alcohol because it can be purchased in higher concentrations of alcohol.

When taken internally, tinctures may have different benefits to the body. Around the house, they can be useful in room fresheners and other sprays.

To make a tincture, take a bunch of fresh plant cuttings and push them down into a glass canning jar, then pour in enough alcohol to completely cover the plant matter. You can fit a surprising amount of plant in one of those jars, so to get a potent tincture, really stuff it in there. Just be sure to completely cover the plants with liquid: If they are exposed to the air, they can grow mold. Then be sure to label your jars with the date and a description of exactly what you put in it, like this: "July 2021, mugwort and vodka." Put the jar somewhere that it isn't near direct sunlight and won't get too warm. After at least a few weeks, remove the plant matter from the tincture by pouring it through a tea strainer. Because they are preserved well by the alcohol, tinctures like this one can last for a good few years. Store them in a dark, dry place.

Decoctions

A decoction is similar to a hot water infusion, but instead of pouring boiling water onto herbs and letting them steep, you place the herbs into the water and then bring it to a boil. This method is generally used for plant material that is of a more woody nature, like bark, which needs heat and the boiling action to release the plant's beneficial properties.

To make a decoction, place one tablespoon per cup of cold, distilled water into a pot. Turn on the burner to medium heat, and cover the pot with a lid. Let it come to a boil, then reduce the heat and let it simmer for about 30 minutes. Keep the lid on the entire time. After about 30 minutes turn off the burner and set the pot aside to cool with the lid still on. Once it has cooled to room temperature, place a strainer over the jar in which you will keep your decoction, and carefully pour in the liquid. Store it in the fridge to prolong its shelf life. Before each use check if you can see a cloudiness in the liquid. If this is present, it indicates that the decoction has turned and it should be thrown away.

Distilled Water

Any recipe in which water will be part of the final product should be made with distilled water, which doesn't contain minerals or other impurities. This can be bought inexpensively, and it's also possible to make it yourself at

Eye of Newt, Toe of Frog

We had the pleasure of visiting the College of Physicians in Philadelphia and learning about the "recipe books" in its collection. These were books that were kept by people, mainly women, from the early modern era up until the mid-19th century. They not only included cooking recipes but ones for creating poultices, ointments, and other treatments for illness and discomfort.

Recipe books were sometimes kept and added to by more than one person, even over generations. In fact, Chrissie Perella, the College's Historical Medical Library Archivist, said that the writers of these books frequently made note within the book of who shared a recipe with them. When one woman's name appears several times in another's recipe book, we know they were likely friends who lived near each other.

These books have more than a little of the witch's grimoire about them, especially the older ones, which blended magic with science and sometimes include rituals that were meant to be performed as the concoction was being made or used. Some of the recipes were entertainingly odd, including the "Oil of Swallows" included in Gervase Markham's *The English House-wife*, published in 1615, which called for the use of up to 20 live swallows. Weird.

home. To do so, you will need a pot with a matching lid and a heatproof bowl just a bit smaller than the interior of the pot. Fill the pot with water about halfway, then place the bowl inside the pot (it should float) and then cover it. Bring the water to a low boil, then turn the heat down slightly. Be sure not to let the water bubble up into the bowl. If it looks like this might happen, turn down the heat more. Water vapor from the boiling water will begin condensing on the lid, then drip down inside the bowl.

We've had the best luck doing this with a pot whose lid has a dome shape. Place the lid on upside down, which will make the condensed water run down toward the center more quickly and efficiently. The water that drips into your bowl is the distilled water. Once the bowl is full, carefully remove it from the pot. Depending on how much distilled water you need you may have to repeat the process.

Conversions

Below are a few conversions you may find useful as you work with recipes. For conversions not listed here, consult an online conversion calculator. Ounces are US fluid ounces.

1 tablespoon = 3 teaspoons

1 fluid ounce = 2 tablespoons

4 ounces = ½ cup

1 teaspoon = ~5 milliliters

.5 fluid ounce = ~15 ml

1 fluid ounce = ~30 ml

Keeping a Grimoire

A grimoire is the quintessential book of magic. For hundreds of years these books have taught curious readers how to cast spells, contact angels, perform alchemy, and more. The spirit of sharing practical information through books has continued on in the more modern instructional guides by and for housekeepers and homemakers. As a kitchen witch, no matter where you fall on the spectrum of practical to magical, a grimoire is a useful tool for keeping yourself organized.

If you're anything like us, you probably have recipes written on little bits of paper in all kinds of random places: inside your bag, stuck to the fridge, or holding your place in the book you're reading. Putting all of these recipes in one spot will make them much easier to find. You could collect them in any number of ways, such as a dedicated notebook, a folder, a binder, or a box. We like the flexibility of a binder. Available in small and large sizes, binders allow you to gather all your notes together. You can rearrange the pages as you like and add more as needed. Try punching holes in loose pages and collecting others in folders. You can have great fun decorating your folders and even the binder itself with collages, drawings, or stickers.

Organize your binder by season, ingredient, section of the house, day and evening routines—whatever makes the most sense to you. If you have a garden, make a section for that. Keep track of when you planted seeds, when they sprouted, and plans for the garden layout. Include sketches of the plants if you are so inclined. Perhaps you do a daily tarot card reading; notes about that could go in your tarot or daily rituals section.

Your collection of recipes is always a work in progress, so there's no need to worry about it being perfect. In fact, that's kind of the point. Add recipes as you learn them and annotate them whenever you think of something new. If an ingredient or technique you tried on your third—or three hundredth—attempt works better for you, make a note of it for the future. And if you remember, include the date you first tried or updated a recipe. This will be useful to you as you go back to make changes and additions.

A digital grimoire might be practical for those who prefer to work without paper. A folder of browser bookmarks for reputable blogs, digitized books, and websites can serve as your scrapbook. So can a folder of your own documents that lives on your computer or tablet.

However you choose to organize your working grimoire, you can create a more formal version once you have an assortment of recipes and things that you want to keep forever and perhaps share with others. This could take the form of a beautiful notebook with handwritten text, or a zine you design and print yourself. The book you're holding in your hands right now is our grimoire, and we're happy to think of it living on a shelf in your home, too.

Cleaning

House

Introduction

by Katie

My journey to making my own household cleaners started several years ago, when I met a lovely young artist named Melba at a zine fair. In exchange for some of my self-published zines, she gave me a few special gifts: A plant she'd propagated, a small terrarium, and a tall glass jar filled with homemade liquid laundry soap. She wrote the ingredients on a paper tag she attached to the jar: castile soap, borax, washing soda, and lavender essential oil. The soap smelled lovely and I used it for a good few months until it was gone. I didn't try making my own laundry soap right away, but this homemade batch was a revelation to me. *I could do it myself.*

The next year, for Christmas, my mother gave me a book on safe and healthful household cleaning techniques called *The Organically Clean Home* by Becky Rapinchuk, along with a small collection of essential oils. It ended up being one of the best gifts I've ever received. By this time my husband Joe and I were living in a 100-year-old house in the city, a place I really loved. I enjoyed working to keep it bright and clean, but disliked the harsh smell of the cleaners I bought at the supermarket. I must have complained about this to my mother, whose gift was a gentle reminder that there are other ways to approach the problem. Once I had this book in my hands I was able to recreate Melba's laundry soap, and I started to understand that I had more power and choice than I'd realized. I began trying different recipes and asking people for advice, gradually incorporating more and more natural techniques into my daily routine. In the years since I started on this path I have gotten a ton of satisfaction out of cleaning my home and knowing that it's safe and healthy for me, Joe, and our dear cat Coco.

I have also done a fair amount of research on this subject over the last few years, and it has been both illuminating and frequently disturbing. One thing I learned is that many, if not most, commercial cleaning products sold in the store contain chemicals that are neurotoxins. To give just one example, a report published by *National Geographic* revealed that many commercial air fresheners work by using chemicals that deaden the nerves that coat our nasal passages, which temporarily disables our ability to smell the bad smells. I find this almost unbelievably disgusting—not to mention unnecessary, since it's entirely possible to clean and deodorize things gently and safely. Why should these gross corporations get to sell us products that harm us, while they get bigger and richer?

I don't think they should. I think social change begins at home, and that small, personal actions have power. I also think that even the most mundane chores can be done with intention, transforming them into sources of pleasure and pride. The following is a collection of my favorite techniques for keeping your home clean, lovely, and safe.

One-Ingredient Wizardry

by Katie and Nadine

I n the pages that follow we will share a number of recipes, many of which require a few simple ingredients that, when combined, make lovely body care treatments and products to clean your home. However, there are some ingredients that can accomplish quite a bit around the house all on their own. We have compiled them in the list below.

Baking Soda

Baking soda is the ultimate one-ingredient fixer. You probably already know that it excels at absorbing odors but it can be used all over the house. Here are just a few ways to use it:

Leave a box open in the fridge and one in the freezer to absorb the stronger odors given off by foods like fish and onions. Don't throw it away once it has stopped working; put it back in the cupboard to be used for kitchen and bathroom scrubbing.

Rub away those hard water spots that form on chrome taps in the bathroom or shine up stainless steel sinks. Just dampen a cotton cloth, dab some baking soda onto it, and rub it around the metal hardware in your bathroom and kitchen. They'll come up gleaming.

Sprinkle some in a stinky old pair of shoes. (And remember to dump it in the trash before the next time you wear them!)

Paper is notoriously hard to freshen, but you can reliably take at least some of the musty smell out of old books and documents by putting them in a plastic sandwich bag along with some loose baking soda. Leave the bag sealed for a few days.

Distilled White Vinegar

Okay, maybe vinegar is the ultimate one-ingredient fixer. Get yourself some distilled white vinegar—you'll be amazed by how useful it is around the house. It's corrosive, and as such it is good at removing stubborn cooking grease. Try using it to clean your stove's burner covers. Put the stopper in your kitchen sink, set the burners down into it, and pour hot water and vinegar over them. Let them soak like this for a couple of hours. After you scrub and rinse them they should come up clean and smooth.

Vinegar is also great for removing price tags and the sticky gunk they leave behind. Depending on the material you're trying to remove them from, you may not want to soak it. Simply dabbing some onto a cloth and rubbing the sticky substance will often do the trick.

Add up to a cup of vinegar to the wash cycle of your white laundry to lift stains and brighten them. Use it instead of fabric softener to keep your towels fluffy. Doing this could also help your clothes, especially jeans, retain their color.

Vinegar will remove limescale in the bathroom and kitchen. Just soak a rag in the vinegar, then wrap it around the faucet or shower head for a few hours. (Leave it on for longer if you have a serious build-up.) When you remove the rag and wipe down the surface the crud should break up and wipe away.

Vinegar can also kill weeds. On a sunny day, spray it directly on the plant, making sure not to hit anything else growing in the vicinity. Wait a day and spray it again. Repeat as necessary. You can also try boiling water as an alternative to vinegar.

(A word of warning: Never mix vinegar and bleach. The chemical reaction that occurs when they come into contact with each other creates a toxic gas.)

Technically two ingredients

If you combine baking soda and vinegar, you can really get stuff done. Add together equal parts baking soda and vinegar to make an excellent scrubbing paste for removing grime from cooking pots and pans. For really stuck-on or burned messes, like in a baking pan, remove as much of the food remnants as you can. Then cover the bottom of the pan with baking soda and pour on enough vinegar so that the bubbles reach up the sides of the pan. Let this soak overnight, or longer. All that mess should then come off relatively easily with some scrubbing from a sponge and a bit of dish soap.

You can also use this combination to unclog a blocked drain or keep it clear and less likely to clog in the future. Pour about a cup of baking soda in the drain, followed by enough vinegar to make it froth up into the sink a bit. Let that sit for an hour. Don't let any water go down the drain during this time. Then, pour in a few cups of boiling water. If you are trying to remove a clog and these steps did not work, repeat the process.

Castile soap

Castile soap, which is made of plant oils and does not contain sudsing agents, is biodegradable and gentler than other kinds of soaps and detergents, so we feel good about using it all over the house. Try it on your kitchen floor. First fill two buckets with warm water. In one, add one or two squirts of liquid castile soap, then wash your floors with it. You don't need to use a mop if you don't like them— just dunk a cotton washcloth in the bucket, then use it on the dirty floor. As the rag gets soiled, submerge it in the bucket filled with clean water and wring it out.

Citric acid

Citric acid will remove hard water marks on toilets, and it will banish mold and bacteria too. It's a miracle fix! Just shake some of the crystals into the bowl, then rub them onto the stains with a rag. With very little effort you will be able to pull away the deposits left on the porcelain by minerals in your water, leaving the bowl clean and white again.

To remove tea stains and oily coffee residue from the interior of teapots and coffee pots, sprinkle in one to two tablespoons of citric acid and then fill the pot about halfway up with water. Swirl the water around in the pot. Eventually you should see tea stains lifting and the coffee pot looking cleaner. Dip a sponge (that does not have any dish soap on it) into the citric acid water and use that to scrub stubborn spots and to wipe down the exterior of the pot. Rinse well.

Green tea

We once read that sprinkling green tea over the litter in the cat box helps absorb odors, and it really does. Of course it's no substitute for scooping the box out daily and giving it a more thorough cleaning on a regular basis, but in the hot summer months it helps keep things from getting too wild in there. Buy some inexpensive green tea, and when the situation calls for it, cut open a tea bag and sprinkle the leaves over the litter. The tea helps to neutralize bad smells rather than mask them.

Try placing a bag of green tea into any drawers that smell musty. It absorbs stale odors there too.

Lavender

During the middle ages people threw herbs onto the floors of their houses as a way to introduce fragrances into the home, and also perhaps to ward off pests. As an homage to this antiquated practice of herb strewing, toss a few handfuls of dried lavender flowers onto a rug before vacuuming it. Crush the flowers a bit in your hands first to release their scent, or walk on them once they're on the floor. Let the flowers sit for maybe half an hour or more, then vacuum the rug. A light lavender scent will waft around briefly via the vacuum cleaner's filters. This is a nice way to freshen up a room you would vacuum right before guests arrive or as the very last step in your cleaning routine, especially if your vacuum cleaner sometimes emits a less-than-appealing odor of pet hair and dust.

Lemon

If you have a garbage disposal in your kitchen sink, you know how easily it can get clogged. Here's a preventative tip that came directly from the company that repaired Katie's garbage disposal when it was backed up: Throw a lemon wedge in there every so often and grind it up. The acidity of the lemon can help cut through greasy clogs before they get too serious.

Rubbing alcohol

This is a truly excellent way to get windows and other glass surfaces clean and shining. It's Katie's mom's old trick and it works like a charm. Put equal amounts of rubbing alcohol and water in a spray bottle, spray it directly onto the glass, and buff it clean and dry with a cotton cloth. Use more alcohol than water for especially grimy situations. The alcohol will evaporate very quickly, but do this kind of cleaning on a day when you can keep the windows open for a short while afterward, as it's not healthy to breathe in a lot of it.

Lovely Liquid Laundry Soap

by Katie

This simple, perfect recipe is the one that got me hooked on making my own cleaning supplies. I first made it by following the instructions in Becky Rapinchuk's excellent book, *The Organically Clean Home*. I can whole-heartedly recommend using the recipe that appears in her book, but here is the version I've come up with by making some adjustments that work for me.

This recipe makes a yield of 64 ounces, or 8 cups, of laundry soap.

You will need:

1.25 oz of liquid castile soap (about 1.5 tablespoons)

1/4 cup borax

1/4 cup washing soda

Cooking pot

Wooden spoon

64-ounce (8-cup) container for storage

Measure 1.25 ounces of liquid castile soap in a measuring cup, then pour it into your pot.

I like Dr. Bronner's castile soap, which comes in an unscented version as well as a variety of naturally scented ones. Next add the borax and washing soda, with a splash of water to soften the powders a bit. Heat the mixture on a low heat until the powders are totally dissolved, stirring continually with your wooden spoon; otherwise the mixture will stick to the pot. The contents of the pot will get all frothy and smooth when they're properly mixed.

Now turn off the burner so that the mixture is no longer heating up. If you want to scent your soap, add several drops of essential oils now and stir them in. Pour the soap mix from the pot into a container with a lid, then fill it the rest of the way with hot water from the tap (not boiling). I use a tall glass canning jar that holds 64 fluid ounces, which is the total yield of this recipe.

Give the jar a good shake before you use the soap each time. Somewhere between a quarter and a half cup of the mixture works well for a regular-sized load of laundry, but I usually just eyeball it.

"It's About Thyme" Countertop Cleaner

by Katie

You may already know how useful vinegar is around the house. It shines up surfaces beautifully, and it contains acetic acid so it also works as a disinfectant. I keep a large bottle of distilled white vinegar underneath my sink alongside all my other cleaning tools—rags, cooking pot, rubber gloves, and so forth—and use it frequently.

Now, I don't at all dislike the smell of vinegar, but it is very *foody*. Despite the fact that I use it for cleaning just about every day, it tends to remind me of fish and chips rather than gleaming countertops. To sweeten the scent of this simple but oh-so-effective cleaner, make an herbal vinegar infusion.

The thyme plant is antimicrobial and has been proven to inhibit salmonella, which makes it a great candidate for a cleaning solution. If you have thyme growing, cut a few sprigs. If you don't, a trip to the supermarket should solve the problem: In the produce section of many grocery stores you'll find fresh-cut herbs in bundles. Pick up a bottle of distilled white vinegar while you're there, and you're ready to go.

Altogether you will need:

Fresh or dried thyme sprigs
Distilled white vinegar
Glass canning jar, parchment paper, and a rubber band
Label

Strainer or cheesecloth
Spray bottle

Following the infusion instructions detailed in *Infusions, Tinctures, and Decoctions* (page 45), press the thyme down into the jar about halfway, then pour in enough distilled white vinegar to fill the jar the rest of the way up, completely covering the thyme. Dried herbs will work for infusions too—in fact, you can use a smaller quantity of these. For fresh-cut herbs use about twice as much vinegar, and for dried herbs use about 15 times as much.

Cover the jar with a lid that isn't made of metal because the vinegar will corrode and rust it. A piece of coated paper held on with a rubber band does the trick. Don't forget to label your jar with the date and contents.

Scents and Sensibility

For some people, being in public can mean having a serious allergic reaction or illness triggered by other people's perfumes or laundry detergents, plug-in air "fresheners," and other fragrances. Reactions can include sneezing, dizziness, fainting, skin rashes, asthma, and headaches. I am a longtime migraine sufferer, and strong scents—especially artificial, added fragrances— are one of my triggers. If you're wearing a lot of perfume, I'm crossing the street!

I like to add essential oils to some of the cleaning products I use around the house, both for the scent and for any disinfecting properties the plant has, and you can scent your laundry soap this way, too. Essential oils will make the fragrance much milder than an artificially scented detergent. But to be truly mindful of the people you come into contact with when you leave the house, using an unscented laundry soap is the way to go.

Once you've done all this, put the jar in a cool, dark place for at least two weeks. When I made a batch of this infusion recently, I took it out after two weeks and gave it a sniff and decided I wanted it to be stronger, so I put it back on the shelf for another week.

When the infusion is ready it will have a pale yellow color and a wonderful scent. Strain the plant matter out from the vinegar using a kitchen strainer or a piece of cheesecloth. Then pour the liquid into a spray bottle. If there is any left over, store it in a jar for future use. Vinegar infusions have a shelf life of around six months.

To use, simply spritz the cleaner onto a cotton rag or directly onto the counter or other surface and mop it up. Go ahead and use it to clean your dish drying rack: It will cut right through the gunk that can accumulate on there. Don't use this spray on granite, marble, or soapstone surfaces as the acidity of the vinegar can damage them over time.

Peppermint Pest Control

by Katie

I don't know what's going on with the ants in this house. We seem to get them every summer, which is common, but this past year we saw them in the house during the winter months, too. Most often we get tiny household ants, but we also briefly had an infestation of black fire ants, and those suckers bite!

Full disclosure: To combat this problem we first put out commercial ant bait traps, which contain a pesticide. They either worked only a little or not at all. Over the following several weeks, more ants kept getting into the house, and we'd find them on the kitchen counters, the kitchen table, and the kitchen *walls*. One afternoon I had a disgusting surprise waiting for me when I saw that many, many ants had found their way into, but not out of, a jar of honey.

Since I'd always heard that peppermint is effective in keeping ants away, I took this route next. I bought a big bottle of peppermint essential oil and cut sprigs of mint from my garden. I wiped the peppermint oil along the base of the back door and stuffed a wad of cotton saturated with the oil in a spot next to the door where I suspected they were getting in. After the honey incident, I also wiped the oil around the perimeter of the baking cabinet and put some sprigs on the cabinet's shelf. I didn't see another ant in the cabinet after that, and though some continued to get into the house for a short while, that soon stopped too, leaving our house happily ant-free. Perhaps the traps helped, but the peppermint gave a quicker, more satisfying result.

For best results, wash the spots where the ants are getting in with soapy water to remove their scent trail before putting down the essential oil, and re-apply the oil as needed. You will likely have to do both steps several times. Also, this method works better if you're vigilant before the problem has gotten out of hand.

The science behind this approach has to do with the way ants communicate with each other. The insects use chemical scent signals to leave a trail for each other, and once an ant has found food or a safe place to live, it will leave a pheromone trail for the others to follow. A negative chemical signal will work the opposite way and repel them. Mint oil is one of several ant repellents used by people who practice Integrated Pest Management, an approach to controlling "pests" that is less hazardous to human beings and other creatures because it uses non-chemical tools first and is based on an understanding of the insect or animal's behaviors. Other herbal ant repellents include rosemary, clove, orange, and thyme.

Bathroom Brightening Scrub

by Katie

When it comes to cleaning the toilet, sink, tub, and other surfaces in your bathroom, gentle scrubbing methods work best. The first bathroom scrub I ever made was from a recipe in a book called *Herbal Home Hints* by Louise Gruenberg. It called for baking soda, borax, and washing soda, plus some disinfecting essential oils. Other folks swear by different combinations of two of these three powders. My preferred method uses washing soda and borax, with a few carefully chosen oils.

Try using:

1 part washing soda

1 part borax

Essential oils

Coffee can or shaker bottle

Rubber gloves

Measure out the washing soda and borax in equal amounts. For a recent small batch of scrub—enough to clean my bathtub twice, the bathroom sink three times, and the toilet once—I used one-third cup of washing soda, one-third cup of borax, and five drops each of tea tree, rosemary, and orange oils. I suggest making and then storing this scrub in an empty coffee can or the shaker bottles that grated cheese comes in, which are excellent for sprinkling the scrub. First put the powders in there, then drop in your essential oils. Once all of your ingredients are in the container, close and shake it to mix them together. This product keeps fresh for a long time, so feel free to make a larger quantity of it if that's what works for you.

There are a number of different essential oils with disinfectant properties, and as far as I'm concerned you can more or less tell which ones they are by smelling them. Imagine the clean, sharp, almost medicinal scent of rosemary, thyme, tea tree, and eucalyptus, and you'll understand what I mean. Peppermint, lavender, and citrus oils are germ-fighting as well. One of my favorite blends for cleaning the bathroom is equal parts tea tree oil, rosemary essential oil, and sweet orange essential oil. Tea tree oil is antibacterial, antifungal, and antiviral, and rosemary and orange oil are both antibacterial. I absolutely love rosemary for cleaning and I never get tired of its comforting smell.

To use, simply sprinkle a small quantity of the scrub onto a wet sponge or rag, or directly onto the surface. (Using it liberally is more trouble to clean up, and you don't need much anyway.)

Get the cleaner and the rag nice and wet as you work, and with a little rubbing you will easily lift any stains and stickiness left behind by soap. This scrub is very effective at cleaning porcelain tubs, sinks, and toilets, as well as the fiberglass some bathtubs are made of (though it's too abrasive to use on grout). Be sure to rinse it away completely afterward, especially since in the near future you'll be soaking your lovely bod in those tubs and sinks.

To be on the safe side, open the window for ventilation and always wear rubber gloves while you work. Gloves will protect your skin from the tea tree oil, which could be irritating in large doses, as well as from gnarly bathroom germs.

After cleaning and rinsing with a wet cloth, buff the surface with a dry cloth. This will prevent any powdery residue from being left behind and will leave surfaces gleaming. When all you need to do is shine up those ugly spots that get left behind on metal taps by hard water, baking soda on its own does the job just as well.

Another tip: If you have hard water—that is, water with a lot of naturally-occuring minerals in it—you may notice funky brown stains forming on the toilet bowl around and underneath the water line that are really hard to budge. Regular cleaning with this scrub will help lift them, but if you have a serious case to start with, try a pumice stone. Yes, like the ones you use on your feet. Hardware stores sell pumice on handles for cleaning the toilet bowl. They work very well and won't scratch the porcelain, no matter how much elbow grease you employ.

Winter Woods Room Spray

by Katie

There's a reason so many commercial cleaning products smell like a forest of evergreen trees. It's one of the freshest scents in nature, and it's strong. Traditionally, juniper cuttings were one of several types of fragrant plants that were strewn around the house to absorb bad smells on the floor and freshen the air.

One winter I received an evergreen-scented room spray as a gift. My friend had bought it for me at a craft market, and the mysterious, amber-colored bottle was marked only with a beautiful, handmade tag that said "juniper berry and fir." I loved the scent during the winter season and later found that I enjoyed it just as much in the warmer months, so I began experimenting with making my own forest-fresh blend.

This recipe makes about two ounces of air freshener. I recommend using it in the bathroom because its bracing scent completely banishes any bad smells that might be lingering in there.

Ingredients:

15 milliliters (~.5 fluid ounces) grain alcohol, at least 151-proof
1.75 milliliters (54 drops) essential oils
42.25 milliliters (~1.5 fluid ounces) distilled water
Medicine measuring cup
2-ounce spray bottle

Using a medicine measuring cup, measure out .15 milliliters of the grain alcohol (I use Everclear). The medicine measuring cup makes this easier since it has smaller measurements than kitchen measuring cups do. Next add 1.75 milliliters of essential oils to the alcohol—this comes out to about 54 drops. These measurements are based on the proportions needed to dissolve essential oils before adding them to water. See page 44 for more on solubilization.

For a woodsy scent blend, try 25 drops of cedarwood, 15 drops of juniper berry, 10 drops of silver fir, and 4 drops of lavender essential oils. Since these types of oils can be pricey, you can experiment with using two or three essential oils instead of four, if you prefer; just

Bonus Points: Pine Needle Tincture

Since you need grain alcohol to make this recipe anyway, why not make a pine needle tincture for extra fun? Because the tincture is made with grain alcohol it will dissolve the essential oils in the same way the alcohol does on its own, and it will give the blend an even stronger scent.

If you have a pine tree on your property, take a handful of fresh needles and put them in a glass jar. Pour in enough grain alcohol to cover them, seal the jar with the lid, and let it sit somewhere away from direct sunlight for at least a week. Be sure to label the jar with its contents and the date. When you strain the needles out of the liquid it will be a beautiful pale green color and will carry a strong scent. Then follow the Winter Woods recipe using the tincture in place of the grain alcohol.

be sure it adds up to 54 drops total. One of my favorite two-scent combinations is silver fir and Atlas cedarwood. Silver fir smells softer than some of the more intense evergreens, and cedarwood, though woody, also has a decidedly sweet note. Together they make a fresh blend that's both bright and fragrant. If there is a shop near you that sells essential oils, I recommend going there and having a sniff fest. The sense of smell is a powerful one, and when you find fragrances that you like and that go well together, you'll know it.

Cover your alcohol and essential oil mixture and let it sit for a few hours to properly dissolve before adding the water. You'll be able to see that the oils are dissolving because they'll make the liquid look cloudy. The last time I made this spray I let the essential oils sit in the alcohol for around four hours while I went out and ran errands. By the time I got back home the oils looked like they'd broken down into the alcohol thoroughly, so I added the distilled water then.

The water should make up 75 percent of the total mixture minus the amount of essential oil you added. In this case, that comes to 42.25 milliliters of water. Pour the completed concoction into a spray bottle, and *voilà*! You're ready to start spritzing.

Witchy Crafts

*A*s kitchen witches, we love and honor the idea of the *hearth*, the home we create for ourselves by making things with intentionality and love. Using a few simple techniques, you can make a variety of useful crafts and decorations for your space.

Knit a Dishcloth

by Katie

My mother taught me how to make these knitted dishcloths a long time ago. The pattern is a pleasure to work and it knits up in just a few hours. If you're an experienced knitter you can make variations on this pattern that have pretty designs in the middle—and if you've never knitted anything before in your life, this would make a good first project. It's simple and small, and since it's not a piece of clothing that needs to be exactly the right size, it's very forgiving.

These dishcloths look pretty in the kitchen and last for years, and they've saved many trees from being turned into the paper towels I don't use! I like to spray them with the "It's About Thyme" Countertop Cleaner (page 67) and use them to wipe down tables and counters. They also make good washcloths for your face.

When I asked my mother for the original pattern to include in this book, she said: "Sure, I'll share it, but this isn't really my pattern. I got it from Aunt Lynda, who was always a great knitter—and who knows where she got it from." When she said this, I instantly got a mental image of the blueberry festivals and church bazaars we'd go to when we were up in Maine visiting family, where these types of hand-knitted items were always sold. My aunt and my uncle lived in rural Maine for many years, on a few different tiny homestead farms, and they always kept some animals, including sheep. Aunt

Lynda would have the sheep sheared, then spin their wool into yarn and use it for all kinds of projects. When it came to simple living she was an inspiration to my mother—who, incidentally, is also a great knitter—and to me, once I was old enough to be interested in such things.

And as for not knowing where her knitting pattern came from, well, that's kind of the nature of these things, isn't it? Simple, useful patterns get handed down over the generations, with alterations being made as the knitter sees fit. Here is the pattern my Aunt Lynda gave my mom some 40 years ago now, along with some additional tips of my own.

You will need:

Knitting needles in size 7 or 8. Pick these up at any craft supply store, or see if someone you know has a pair. Knitting needles come in plastic, aluminum, and bamboo. I prefer using plastic or bamboo needles because I find they let the yarn move more smoothly than the aluminum ones do, but this is a personal preference.

Cotton worsted weight yarn. One skein is good to start; you should be able to get a couple of dishcloths out of that. Be sure to buy 100% cotton yarn since you'll be getting these cloths wet and using them to clean, and wool and acrylic aren't suitable for that. *Worsted weight* refers to the thickness of the yarn; it is also sometimes called *medium weight*. My favorite line of cotton yarns is the one my mother has always used: Sugar'n Cream by Lily. It's inexpensive, comes in tons of colors, and is easily found at craft supply stores.

This pattern creates a square-shaped cloth with a border around the edges. As you knit, the washcloth will "grow" from one corner to the opposite one. For the first half of the pattern you'll be increasing the number of stitches per row, and for the second half you'll decrease them.

First wind your skein of yarn into a ball to keep it from tangling while you work. Then cast on 2 stitches.

Row 1: knit 1, yarn over, knit 1

Row 2: knit 1, yarn over, knit to end of row

Repeat row 2 until 46 stitches are on the needle

Next row: knit 2 together, yarn over, knit 2 together, knit to end of row

Repeat this row until 3 stitches remain

Last row: knit 2 together, knit 1. Fasten off by tying a knot.

If you'd like your dishcloth to have a thicker border, cast on 3 instead of 2, then:

Row 1: knit 2, yarn over, knit 1

Row 2: knit 2, yarn over, knit to end of row

Repeat Row 2 until you have 46 stitches on needle

Next row: knit 1, knit 2 together, yarn over, knit 2 together, knit to end of row

Repeat this row until you have 2 or 3 stitches left on the needle, then fasten with a knot.

Wool Dryer Balls and Pet Toys

by Nadine

Using tennis balls to fluff up laundry in the dryer is an old trick. The balls bounce around among the items, enabling heat to move more efficiently. This speeds up drying time and softens fabric. Unfortunately, tennis balls are made of plastic. You can buy an environmentally friendly alternative—wool dryer balls—or you can make them yourself.

For this project you will need wool roving, which is wool that has been brushed and cleaned but not yet spun into yarn. Roving's fluffy, almost cotton candy texture makes it easy to form into a ball quickly and creates a smooth surface on the finished ball. The hot water of the washer and the heat of the dryer will cause the wool fibers to shrink and stick to themselves. This process is called felting. You can find roving in the felting or spinning section of yarn stores.

Roving comes in many lovely colors, but to keep things as natural as possible I prefer the undyed variety. To ensure that you have enough for three balls I recommend starting with three ounces of roving. Honestly, though, one ounce will probably make more than one ball. I first bought six ounces and have made well over six balls, but I want to give you a rough number to start with. If you find yourself drowning in roving, remember these little wooly spheres make lovely gifts.

You will need:

Wool roving

An old pair of pantyhose or old socks (neither should have holes)

Essential oils (optional)

Take a strand of roving and start wrapping it around itself to form a ball. It helps to tie a knot at the end to create a base and then work around that. This is a sort of fiddly task that might seem tedious at first, but stick with it. Keep wrapping the wool around itself tightly. The ball should feel dense, not fluffy like a cotton ball. Since the ball will shrink, aim to make it about the size of a softball. Tear the roving from the skein and tuck the end securely into the ball. Make the ball as smooth as possible to help ensure it will felt together nicely.

Take an old pantyhose or sock and carefully stuff the ball inside. Tie a knot in the hose/sock directly over top of the ball, securing it down tightly. Depending on how long your pantyhose/sock is, you can add more balls, tying a tight knot after each one.

Drop the pantyhose/sock into a load of laundry with hot water.

Drop the pantyhose/sock into the dryer along with the laundry.

At this point the balls should be felted. Repeat steps 3 and 4 if you are unsure, but most likely they have come out just fine. Snip the pantyhose/socks next to the knots and carefully peel the fabric away from the wool. They're ready to use!

Essential Oils: While some people scent their wool dryer balls with essential oils, others warn against doing this because essential oils are flammable and since a dryer gets hot, the essential oils could ignite and start a fire. I have used essential oils on my dryer balls without any problems, but you must decide for yourself if you think this is worth the risk. If you do decide to try it, make sure you do not use essential oils that are pre-mixed with carrier oils. Carrier oils are much more likely to catch fire, plus they can stain laundry. If you do want to try essential oils, apply just a few drops and wait for them to fully absorb into the wool before using the ball. Then keep the dryer heat on low, and do not leave the house while the dryer is running.

Please note that essential oils will most likely not transfer their fragrance onto laundry. A pleasant scent will greet you when you open the dryer door, but that's about the extent of it.

Wool Balls For Pets

To make a ball for a pet, simply follow the instructions for dryer balls and alter the size to suit your pet: smaller for cats, larger for large dogs. As with dryer balls, I prefer to use undyed roving. Of course, do not use essential oils on these pet toys. However, for cats you could experiment with rolling them in catnip, or perhaps store them in a jar with catnip to infuse the wool with its intoxicating scent.

In my dog's toy box I keep a set of three wool balls, which we use for playing catch in the living room when it's too wet or cold to play outside. While the balls do get dirty over time, they somehow never acquire a gross odor like his other toys do. If he gets some fibers in his mouth and swallows them I don't need to be concerned, because it's not like he's eating plastic strings or polyester stuffing. It's only wool. Plus, since he's a herding dog, it's cute to see him chase after little white balls of wool as if they were tiny runaway sheep.

To clean a wool ball, hand-wash it in very warm water with a mild detergent and rinse well. Re-shape the ball into a sphere as you're squeezing out the excess water, then put it in the dryer along with a load of laundry. If a ball has started to unravel, reform it into a tight sphere and then wash and dry it inside a pantyhose/sock as if you were making it for the first time.

Once a wool ball has completely come apart and you want to get rid of it, tear or cut it up and place the fluffy tufts (discarding any pieces that smell like essential oil) outside for birds to use as nesting material. You can put them on the ground near other potentially appealing materials, such as dried flower stalks; drape them over hedges; or enclose them in some kind of container with holes, like those rectangular suet holders, and hang it up where birds can see it. If birds don't seem interested in the wool, put it into your compost.

"Keep out the Cold" Draft Stopper

by Katie

I have lived in apartments with old, rickety window frames and in houses with brand new doors that weren't hung quite right. Both of these situations can lead to a draft on a cold day. The larger the gap, the colder you'll get!

Once I owned my own place I became much more aware of what it costs to heat it, and I didn't want any of that nice, warm air to escape. My husband reminded me of the draft stoppers his mother has always used: Long fabric tubes in cute designs that she would place on the floor along the length of the door. You've seen them, I'm sure. Many have funny slogans on them or are shaped like animals. I made mine in the simplest way possible, using fabric in a design I like so it looks cute too.

You will need:

Fabric of your choice
Needle and thread (or sewing machine)
Rice, sand, or pine needles

You can use any fabric you've got on hand, go to the craft store and browse around, or even tear up a piece of old clothing you can't use anymore. It doesn't matter what type of material you use as long as it has a tight enough weave to keep the contents in. Also keep in mind that the stopper will be sitting on the floor or windowsill, and a lighter color fabric will show dirt sooner.

Measure your door or window, then cut the fabric to that length, plus about two inches. Make it about four inches wide. Fold the strip of fabric in half, lengthwise, with the front side facing in, then sew the long side and one short side shut. When you've finished, pull the fabric strip right-side out through the open end.

Now fill the draft stopper. I use rice but you can also use sand or pine needles. The idea is for the finished product to be hefty but pliable, so that you can bend it and sort of mush it into place. Use a funnel to pour the contents into it so you don't make a mess. If you don't have a funnel, make a temporary one by rolling a piece of paper into a funnel shape. Fill your stopper up to about an inch or two from the top. If you're like me you'll just tie a knot in the top of the fabric, but if you'd rather it look more finished you can sew it shut instead.

At the end of the season, open the stopper back up, pour out its contents, and wash the fabric in the sink or the washing machine. Lay it flat to air dry so it won't shrink or lose its shape. Put it away until you need it again next winter.

Herbal Furniture Freshener

by Katie

I purposely didn't call this chapter "sachets" because I suspect that the idea of a sachet might sound fussy and old-fashioned to you hip kitchen witches. But here's the thing. I have an old bureau in my bedroom that's a hand-me-down from my parents. It's the only piece of furniture I own that I remember from my childhood, and I love it, but it tends to have a persistent musty smell. Whenever I let a piece of clothing sit in the dresser for a couple months or more it would smell stale when I took it out, so I got into the habit of washing those things again before wearing them because the smell bothered me.

Hold on, I thought, after doing this an embarrassing number of times. I have a garden full of fresh herbs, a cabinet full of dried ones, and enough essential oils to drown a fairy. Surely I could use these things to absorb any stale odors and leave behind nice ones. I got over myself and made some sachets, and I've been very happy with the results.

To make your thoroughly modern sachet, you will need:
Any breathable fabric
Needle and thread (or sewing machine)
Dried herbs
A length of twine, yarn, or ribbon
Essential oils (optional)

Get some fabric with a breathable weave. I used unbleached cotton muslin because I happened to have it on hand, and I like its simple, rustic look. Cut your fabric to 8" x 10", then fold it in half and sew the two sides shut, leaving the top open. Push the fabric bag inside out, fill it with your dried herb mixture, and instead of sewing the top shut, tie it with yarn, ribbon, or twine. This way, when the scent of your sachet has faded or you want to try a different one, you can easily open it up and replace the materials inside. (Note: If you're not interested in doing a sewing project, the small muslin drawstring bags that are sold for brewing loose tea work just as well.)

I have used several different types of dried herbs and flowers in my sachets, and I'll also sometimes add a drop or two of essential oil for a stronger scent. You can use any flowers or herbs that smell good to you. Lavender, of course, is a classic. Different varieties of lavender flowers are sold in many stores—try the craft store, an herb shop, a local grower, or a trustworthy mail-order source. Another scent that works well in a sachet is a blend of lemon verbena and mint. I had grown these plants myself, so I picked, air dried, and crushed the leaves before putting them in my fabric bag. I also added one or two drops of cedarwood oil, a scent I love and one that seems at home in a wooden piece of furniture.

To refresh your sachet, give it a squeeze once in a while to release the scent of the herbs inside, or open it up and add a few drops of essential oil. In addition to using scented sachets, I'll sometimes also put a few bags of green tea in my dresser to help absorb stale odors.

Dye Fabric the Natural Way

by Katie

People have been dyeing fabrics with flowers and berries for millennia, and they're all over Instagram doing it right now. Why not give it a try? I used flowers to dye the cotton muslin fabric that I later sewed into drawer sachets and found it to be such a rewarding project, I want to share it with you.

There are many different types of flowers, berries, vegetables, and other plant matter you can use to make fabric dyes. To give one example, my friend Helen, an artist who often works with things found in nature, recommends using the skin from an avocado to get a lovely light green color. To save yourself some time and trouble, look for a comprehensive list of plants that create good dyes. The first time I tried dyeing fabric, I collected several bunches of porcelain berries I found growing wild along the river near my house because they had such fabulous colors—cornflower blues, pale purples, Easter-egg pinks. But I found out that the insides of the berries aren't very pigmented, so they didn't create the gorgeous, pastel-colored dye bath I was dreaming of. Instead, the fabric turned a pale, vegetal brown. (Which was still cool though, to be honest.)

On my next try I used the vivid, dark purple flowers that were in bloom on my basil plant, and I ended up with a beautiful, pale pink fabric. It reminded me of an antique handkerchief, the perfect attitude for my herbal sachets.

You will need:

Cotton muslin fabric

1 part distilled white vinegar

4 parts water

Flowers, roughly chopped

To do this project you'll need to use a natural, not synthetic, fabric. I used unbleached cotton muslin. Remember that fabric dyed this way will not be as intense as most clothing sold in stores, which is usually made from synthetic fabric that's been colored with synthetic dyes.

To prepare the fabric, first put one part vinegar to four parts water in a saucepan. This will be the bath that you use to treat your fabric, which will help it take the dye better. (There are other ingredients that can be used this way, including salt, which is often used when dyeing with berries.) Since I wanted to dye just one small piece of fabric, I used one cup of vinegar and four cups of water. Add the fabric to the pot, turn the heat on low, and let the whole thing simmer for an hour.

Now it's time to make the dye bath. While your fabric is being prepared on the stovetop, chop your flowers roughly and put them in a different pot. Add twice as much water to the pot as you have flowers. For this project, I used one cup of basil flowers and two cups of water. Turn on the heat and bring the flowers and water to a boil, then lower the heat and simmer it for an hour. You will be able to see the water taking on the color of the flowers (or any plant matter you use). Strain and then compost the leftover plants. The liquid that is left will be your dye bath.

Put your fabric into the dye bath and simmer it there for at least one hour. The fabric will not come out as bright or dark as the color of the dye bath you create, so simmer and then soak the fabric in the dye for longer if you want a more vibrant result. I let mine simmer for an hour and a half on the lowest heat setting. Add more water as necessary, since the heat will slowly cook off your dye bath. After your fabric has soaked to your liking, remove it with tongs or a fork (it will be hot) and rinse it under cool water.

Make a Seasonal Wreath

by Katie

Many witches—just like people of different faiths around the world—keep altars in their homes. These can take the form of an arrangement of ritual tools; pictures, candles, and objects to commemorate the dead; or other kinds of displays. The altars I make are almost exclusively small collections of natural objects I've found, such as rocks, leaves, flowers or sprigs of herbs, seashells, pieces of tree bark, and any other pretty thing from nature that I might find when I'm out walking. I find it very gratifying to make something beautiful for my home out of nature's leftovers.

My favorite thing to do with foraged natural materials is to make a wreath. I consider these a kind of altar, too, because I use them to honor and celebrate the seasons. Making wreaths at different times of year has a way of helping me feel more deeply connected to my own life: to the animals, trees, and other plants around me, as well as the passage of the seasons. Depending on where you live, you might experience sweltering summers and bitter cold winters every year. Each season brings unique challenges and offers its own beauty. Each is completely necessary to the circle of life. And I love the way the symbolism of the wreath's circular shape chimes with the pagan Wheel of the Year, a calendar of seasonal holidays that reminds us of the cyclical nature of time.

You will need:

Wreath form or length of vine

Flowers, grasses, seedpods, pinecones, fruits, or other plant pieces

Twine, florist's wire, or floral tape

Your wreath can be as simple or as elaborate as you like, and its complexity will be partly determined by the type of wreath form you use. The wreath forms that are sold at the craft store are almost always made from grapevine because it is both flexible and strong. These pre-made ones are inexpensive, and since they're sturdy they can be reused again and again. Alternatively, if you have a vine growing on your property you can make your own form. I have made very rustic and lovely looking wreaths simply by cutting a length of kudzu or bittersweet vine and gently pulling it around into a circular shape, then tying it with twine and letting it dry.

When you picture what you'd like to put on your wreath, think beyond the traditional Christmas wreaths made of holly and boxwood. Imagine your favorite flowers, grasses, and seeds that grow throughout the year. I make wreaths all year long, and I forage the materials in my own yard and in the woods and streets near my house. When I forage for wreaths, my aim is to only use found items that have already fallen to the ground. I also like to include plants from my own garden or dried flowers from a gift bouquet.

When planning your wreath, choose herbs, flowers, or grasses that look beautiful both fresh and dried. If you don't have your own large garden to pick from, perhaps there is a farm nearby that sells flowers. In the summer and autumn I like to visit a small farm local to me, where for $5 I'm allowed to cut 40 stems of flowers. Last autumn I picked cockscomb, zinnias, marigolds, and ageratum, which produces beautiful clumps of tiny, fluffy purple flowers. Since these are all flowers that dry well, I was able to enjoy my small purchase for months.

As winter approaches I gather small fallen pine boughs that I find as I walk around the neighborhood and in the woods, and by the time the winter solstice comes I have enough for a wreath. I also use them to decorate pieces of furniture around the house. Just give these a quick shake and rinse with clean water if you're planning to bring them inside—you don't want to give any unwanted critters or crawlers a free ride into your house.

When arranging these natural elements on the wreath form, I try for a feeling of balance in my composition by tucking some long grasses or bushy pine needles in first, then nestling smaller pieces like a flower or a pine cone on top of them. Try to keep the stems of the flowers long so that you can wiggle them into place. If they're too short or won't stay put, cut a bit of florist's wire or tape and wrap it around the stem, lashing it to the form.

I like to let the plant material dry on the wreath so I can enjoy watching the whole thing change over time, but you can dry the pieces first if you prefer. You can "flash dry" flowers in beads of silica gel to help them retain their color better, but I much prefer to hang them to air dry as I would a bundle of herbs. (See pages 119-120 for instructions on drying herbs). As you experiment with these arrangements you'll start to get a feeling for which plants look attractive and stay relatively intact when dried. For instance, stems with lots of small leaves typically start to look sad quickly, then drop the leaves as they dry. I remove most leaves, especially tiny ones, from their stems before I add them to my wreaths. Reeds, seed pods, and flowers with tight petals all look pretty when they're fresh as well as dried. If you like the look of dried herbs, tuck some in there too. I often put lavender and rosemary in wreaths alongside larger flowers.

I hang my wreaths on the walls as well as the front door and tend to keep adding to them even after they're on display. One of the things I love most about this kind of decorating is that, since it's not store-bought, you're less likely to feel you have to keep the wreath forever. When you grow tired of it, simply remove the natural materials and either share them with the birds or put them on your compost pile, then use the form to start a new wreath next season.

Mind Your Beeswax 1
Wood Balm

by Nadine

Wooden cutting boards and spoons do a lot of hard work in a busy kitchen, getting cut with knives and taking dips in boiling water. Giving them some attention now and then will help to keep them looking their best. For spoons that have become rough with years of use, a good sanding with a fine grit sandpaper refreshes their surface quickly. Both spoons and cutting boards seem to enjoy a good moisturizing treatment, as they can get dry with constant use and washing. Food-grade mineral oil is usually recommended for this task, but since it is a byproduct of the fossil fuel industry, we don't like to use it in our "natural" kitchens.

The following recipe has just two ingredients. While you can use an oil all by itself, there is a chance it could turn rancid after it has soaked into the wood. The beeswax in the balm should prevent this from happening as it may help preserve the oil somewhat, and it should also keep the oil more on the surface of the wood. Presumably you will be washing these items frequently and therefore removing the balm over time anyway. Always use fresh oil in your balm and give the balm a sniff before applying to make sure it still smells okay. This recipe calls for walnut oil, just because it's often used in woodworking. Be sure to use the food-grade oil found in the grocery store, not the stuff from the hardware store. If anyone in your household has a nut allergy, try a different kind of oil, like olive or avocado, instead.

You will need:

2 tablespoons beeswax

3 tablespoons walnut oil

Yield: 5 tablespoons or 2.5 ounces

Melt the beeswax and oil together in a double boiler, then pour the mixture into a tin or short glass jar. Let it cool completely before putting on the lid. The above recipe makes a small amount of balm, but it should be enough for a couple spoons and a cutting board.

To use, apply the balm with a rag or your hands and rub it into the (clean and dry) wood. Let it sit for at least an hour (or until it feels relatively dry) and then buff it with a clean rag. Wait several hours, or better yet a whole day, to allow the balm to really settle in before using the item. Reapply as often as needed.

Alternative use: If it turns out you don't like what this balm does for wood, try it as an intensive moisturizer for dry skin, especially on the hands.

Mind Your Beeswax 2
Scented Beeswax Melt

by Nadine

I f you have beeswax and there's an electric wax warmer in your home, why not make some scented beeswax melts?

A wax warmer acts like an electric scented candle. Inside a decorative container sits a small light bulb. On top of the container rests a dish that holds a piece of wax, usually called a tart or melt, that melts from the heat of the light bulb. The light peaks through the perforations in the container and the scent from the wax wafts around the room. It's not a perfect imitation of a candle as it does not create the same kind of ambiance, but it certainly is a lot safer than an open flame.

To make these extremely simple melts, all you need is some beeswax and essential oils. Please note that no matter what essential oil you choose, the scent of the beeswax will always come through. Melt the wax in a double boiler, turn off the heat, and then add the desired essential oils. Pour the wax into molds, such as a metal muffin pan or paper cupcake wrappers. Because beeswax requires a higher temperature to turn into a liquid compared to the usual waxes used in commercial wax tarts, make yours relatively thin so that they can melt quickly and evenly in the warmer. Let the wax cool to room temperature and then stick the molds in the freezer to help them pop out easily. They should be frozen in about an hour.

To remove the wax melts from a hard mold like a muffin pan, turn it upside down and tap it firmly against the counter. A paper cupcake wrapper can simply be torn away from the wax. If the wax breaks into pieces during the removal process, don't worry. It's all going to be melted down anyway, and it doesn't have to look pretty to smell good.

To use, simply place the melt into the wax warmer dish and turn on the light. If you find that once your melt has liquified the scent is not as strong as you like, you can add a few more drops of essential oil to the liquid wax. In theory, you could use one piece of wax like this perpetually, just adding more drops of essential oil as the scent fades with use.

Mind Your Beeswax 3
Kitchen Wraps

by Katie

Beeswax-coated fabric wraps are such a nice way to wrap food or cover containers of food. They can be used and reused many times, and when they're no longer useful they'll break down naturally in a compost heap. They're fun to make, too. And since beeswax has antiviral and antibacterial properties, it's an excellent choice for keeping food fresh.

I learned how to create these beeswax food wraps at a workshop taught by Philadelphia-based crafter extraordinaire, Melissa Manna. The class was held in a small public garden in the city in the early evening, at the tail-end of the growing season in October. Melissa set up an ironing board for us to work on right there in the garden. The air was chilly but there were autumn flowers in bloom all around us, and we spotted a tiny mouse hopping through the undergrowth. *Witchy* is the word.

Melissa told me that she'd already been using beeswax to make deodorants and other beauty products for some time when it occurred to her that she could probably make her own food wraps with it as well. Once she saw how well hers came out, she quit buying them and incorporated the project into her DIY repertoire. Here is the method she taught me, along with my own tweaks.

You will need:

Cotton fabric

Beeswax (either a block or pastilles)

Jojoba or almond oil

Pine rosin

Parchment paper

Iron and ironing board

Old towel

Pinking shears

Kitchen grater, if working with a block of beeswax

Only use cotton fabric for this project, in any color and design you like, and be sure it's been washed and dried first. Cut your fabric to whatever size you'd like your wrap to be. Use a ruler and chalk to mark a rectangular shape, or trace a bowl for a circular wrap. Use pinking shears to make your cuts, since fabric cut on a straight edge will eventually start to fray.

Grate your brick of beeswax with a food grater (You can skip this step if you're using beeswax pastilles.) Melissa prefers to use a grater set aside for this purpose. Make enough shavings that, when they're spread out on the fabric, they will cover it evenly. Don't spread them all the way to the edges; instead leave a space of a couple of inches around each side.

Cover your ironing board with an old towel or other fabric you don't mind messing up with beeswax. This will protect the board from any wax that might spill out the sides. Now cut two sheets of parchment paper around twice the size of your fabric, and place one on the ironing board. Lay the fabric down flat on top of it. Spread the beeswax shavings on top of the side of the fabric you want to coat.

Next add a small number of pine rosin pebbles. The rosin works nicely to give the wrap more "grab," and it keeps the beeswax from getting too dry and crumbly. I suggest using around four small pieces.

Next add several drops of oil to the beeswax to make the wrap softer and more pliable. Jojoba oil is a good choice because it's antibacterial, but any food-safe oil will do. Melissa suggests placing one drop of oil on each of the four corners of the fabric and one in the middle. This should be enough, but you can add more as needed.

Now cover this whole thing with the other sheet of parchment paper. Turn your iron to its highest temperature, making sure it's not set to steam. Then simply press the iron down on the middle of the parchment paper for a moment, and you'll be able to see, through the paper, that the beeswax is melting. The fabric will appear wet as it gets covered by the wax. Press and slide the iron around evenly over the paper until you can see that all the wax has melted and has covered every bit of the fabric. Some of the melted wax might run out past the edge of the fabric, which is fine—you cut the parchment paper larger than the fabric for just this reason, to protect the iron from getting wax on it. If you find you haven't grated quite enough beeswax to coat the whole wrap, no big deal. Just pull back the parchment paper and add a bit more. In fact, I have found that it works best to add the shavings or pastilles a few at a time to prevent the beeswax from going on too thick.

Once the fabric is totally covered, your wrap is almost complete. After waiting just a moment you can peel the top sheet of parchment paper away from the fabric, then pull the fabric away from the paper underneath. Pick away any bits of beeswax that have clumped onto the outer edges of the fabric. If you see any spots you missed, just replace the parchment and go over them again with the iron. Once the wrap has cooled and dried for several minutes, it's finished and ready to use. And doesn't it smell gorgeous?

Please note: It's fine to reuse the parchment paper to make more than one wrap, but be very careful to keep the used side facing down. Getting melted beeswax on and in your iron would most likely ruin it.

To use and maintain:

- To cover a container, warm up the wrap a bit in your hands first, then mold it around the container and onto itself. If needed, a rubber band will hold the wrap in place.

- You can use these to wrap any type of food other than raw meat or fish.

- Care for your wraps by rinsing them in cool water and hanging them to dry.

- If you notice that the wrap is getting tired and losing its cling, spruce it up by adding more beeswax and oil in the same way you did when you made it.

These wraps last for about a year. When it's time to retire one, you can cut it up into small pieces and compost it or use it as a firestarter in the fireplace.

In the

Garden

Gardening, even in its simplest forms, provides a powerful connection to the creativity of nature. You don't need a lot of land or resources to grow plants that are useful and beautiful, and newcomers are encouraged to start small. Try growing a windowsill herb garden, freshening the air in your home with houseplants, or experimenting with apartment-friendly household composting.

Growing, Harvesting, and Preserving Herbs

by Katie

> *[A] gardener's magic is about the hopes and fears of men, in love or loveless, terrified or inquisitive, always in trouble of some kind or other, who looked out into the garden for help—and perhaps found it, because they were so sure it must be there.*

> –Bridget Boland, *Gardener's Lore*

The word *herb* is short for *herbaceous plant*. The way most of us use the word, however, does not denote a scientific classification—in common use, herb means "any useful plant." For instance, roses are considered herbs because their petals and fruits can be eaten and used for their healing properties. There is a relatively small number of common herbs, such as the basil and oregano we use in the kitchen, but there are hundreds more that are used not only for cooking but also in medicines and magical preparations.

Long story short, herbs are wonderful. They smell and taste gorgeous, and they've been useful to people for eons. It makes me feel connected to the generations of women who came before me, and I consider it something of a radical act to grow even a modest amount of your own food to enjoy and share with other people.

They're also pretty darn easy to grow. Depending on the type of plant and the place where you live, some can even survive a cold winter outdoors. I have a small, urban backyard in Philadelphia, which is in hardiness zone 7a (You can look up the USDA Hardiness Zone Map online to find out yours). Our outdoor space measures around 340 square feet—not huge—but my partner and I have managed to grow lots of useful plants, mainly herbs and vegetables, on this property. We usually grow a good number of flowers, too. Last summer I went all out. I dug up a new garden bed, around eight by ten feet in size, and planted lots of herbs, both in that space and in containers around it. My goal was to cultivate so many herb plants that my house would look like a witch's cottage, and I think I came close.

Caring for some plants can be involved and challenging—just ask an orchid lover—but herbs tend to be hardy, resilient, and difficult to kill. Even novice gardeners should be able to get plenty of satisfaction out of growing a few of these beautifully scented plants. Whether you keep a small windowsill garden in your kitchen or have ambitions for more and bigger plants, show them lots of love—or, more accurately, the *right amount* of love—and they will reward you with their beauty and usefulness.

Every year I start some plants indoors from seeds during the early spring and then plant them outside in early May, when the last chance of frost has passed. This date varies by region, of course. If you live in a place that gets below freezing in the winter, look up the date of the last chance of frost in your area. Often the plants that start life indoors don't have enough challenges to their survival to properly toughen up, but I always start some this way anyway, for fun. This past growing season I started chamomile, lavender, and chives from seed and only ended up with just two happy little chive plants, which I grew in a pot outside my back door. I was pleased with this tiny yield.

Starting plants from seeds is relatively easy. You can get seeds online or from your local nursery or garden center—or, if you already have an established garden, from your own plants. Besides the seeds, you'll also need some kind of starter material, like coconut fibers, which are also available at garden centers or online gardening suppliers. These coconut fibers, called coir, come in blocks or little pods that need to be soaked in water. This makes the fibers expand, creating a soft material that's ideal for growing seedlings. For the container you can buy plastic trays divided into cells accompanied by clear plastic covers from gardening suppliers, or make your own out of plastic egg cartons.

Radical Herbalism

When information about plants and their uses is collected and published, the resulting book is called an herbal. One of the most important herbals of all time was written and published in 1653 by the English botanist, herbalist, and astrologer Nicholas Culpeper.

There are a few reasons *Culpeper's Herbal*, as it is now known, was so significant. One was its author's political stance. Medicine was rapidly becoming commodified, but he was a radical who believed that traditional knowledge belonged to the people and that they should have unrestricted access to it. In fact, he wrote the *Herbal* in English, not Latin, so that it could be used by people with no formal education. "Jupiter delights in equality, and so do I," he wrote.

In his wonderfully entertaining book, *The Herbalist: Nicholas Culpeper And The Fight For Medical Freedom*, author Benjamin Woolley tells us that Culpeper was raised in an aristocratic family and was slated to become a physician, but he got his earliest lessons in healing from the working women who ran the household. As a little boy, he helped them by picking clary in the churchyard, which they used to strengthen weak backs. A few short years later, instead of studying medicine at Cambridge, he trained as an apprentice to an apothecary in London. There he learned hands-on about plant medicine by treating the city's poor. When he completed his apprenticeship he opened his own dispensary in an area outside of the city, where herbs grew wild, and treated people at little or no cost.

Culpeper also supported the work of midwives, which was women's work that was under threat of being taken over by male authority, and he railed against the ruling classes in general. At one point he was even tried for witchcraft, a crime he could have been given the death penalty for. It's not known who accused him, but most likely it was the physicians who wanted to shut down his practice. In addition to his *Herbal*, he wrote pamphlets that were critical of doctors, priests, lawyers, and even the king. Is it any wonder he's our hero?

1. Plastic egg cartons have three sections, or trays, two of which hold eggs, and one smooth lid that keeps the two egg sections together. Remove the paper label from the lid. Separate the sections by cutting them apart. You now have three trays.

2. Poke a small hole at the bottom of each egg-holding cup of one of the two egg trays. This is for drainage.

3. Fill the poked egg tray with coconut fiber. Place this tray inside the other egg tray, the one without holes. Set this double tray into a shallow baking dish to catch any overflowing water. Place the whole thing near a window that gets sunlight for most of the day.

4. Plant your seeds in the egg tray. If planting different kinds of seeds in the same tray, draw

a diagram of the tray and write down which seeds are in which egg cup.

5. Water the filled tray and place the lid on top. Keep the coconut fiber moist but not soggy.

6. Wait patiently.

7. Admire the tiny seedlings as they hatch out into the sunlight. They are often enveloped in a hazy cloud much like the nebula of a newborn star.

8. Cull excess seedlings from the egg cup, allowing the two or three largest ones to survive.

9. Transfer the seedlings outside, following the guidelines provided on the seed package. This is usually done by a process called "hardening off," in which you set them outside for a longer period of time each day before bringing them back indoors. Once you've done this for around a week they'll be ready to stay out overnight, though the time varies depending on the plant. Then they're ready to be planted in the ground.

If you don't have a greenhouse of your own, I strongly recommend that you also buy small starter plants from a nursery. These will have been started in greenhouses, so they'll be sturdier. Before you begin your garden, ask around to find out which kind of plants grow best in your area. To give you an example of a basic herb garden that can easily be grown in a humid continental or subtropical climate, last summer I planted:

Lavender (*Lavendula* sp.)

Rosemary (*Salvia rosmarinus*)

Thyme (*Thymus vulgaris*)

Dill (*Anethum graveolens*)

Catnip (*Nepeta cataria*)

Oregano (*Origanum vulgare*)

Lemon balm (*Melissa officinalis*)

Mint (*Lamiaceae* sp.)

Tarragon (*Artemisia dracunculus*)

Chives (*Allium schoenoprasum*)

As you can see, most of the herbs I grew are Mediterranean ones that prefer soil that is dry and even poor, so some of them suffered a bit from the excessively rainy summer we had. For instance, the lavender plants both grew huge and lush, but they only grew a few small flowers toward the end of the season, after the rain calmed down. (Happily, the following season the same plants flowered abundantly, and the bees loved them.) In general I keep my gardening expectations low and am pleased with just about anything I can get growing in my yard—including some of the so-called weeds. You never know what Nature has planned, so it's best to keep an open mind.

I've read a lot about growing herbs over the years, but the best lessons I've learned about gardening, I learned by doing. Just dive in and try growing something. Anything! Your results will vary based on where you live and from year to year, but here are a few general tips for successful herb gardening:

- Plant your herbs in rows on the diagonal, to give them more room to grow.

- Mediterranean herbs such as rosemary, parsley, basil, oregano, lavender, and sage, do not like to sit in water. Be sure to provide as much drainage as you can. You can do this by mixing in some gravel or sand with the soil. At the very least, don't overwater them. If you're growing them in containers make sure there are holes in the bottom of the pot where the water can drain out, otherwise the roots will rot and the plant will die.

- In general, herbs love light and a spot with good air circulation. I learned this tip years ago at a workshop led by Jenny Rose Carey, a gardener and educator in the Philadelphia area. I also learned it firsthand in my own herb garden the year my rosemary plant grew wild and huge, which seemed wonderful, but its leaves eventually developed a sticky residue and strong piney scent that I learned were caused by powdery mildew. This can happen to a plant that's kept in hot conditions without enough air circulation. I pruned the plant way back so that it was no longer crowded against the others growing nearby, and after a few weeks the stickiness was almost entirely gone.

- Carey also recommended not enriching your soil with manure or anything else because herbs like soil best when it's "lean and mean," and I have certainly found this to be true. However, I did sprinkle a little of my homemade compost over my new garden this year (see page 122 for more on composting), and the plants responded well to it. You may have to try a few things out before you learn what works best in your own yard, including digging up a plant that's not happy in one spot and seeing how it does in another.

- Many herbs do well indoors and can make great windowsill gardens. They can also be grown in containers outdoors. Remember that it's crucial to water plants in pots more frequently than ones growing in the garden because the shallower soil becomes dry much more quickly.

- Once an herb has flowered, its flavor changes. I tend to let most of my plants flower and do whatever else they feel like doing naturally, in part because I can attract more bees and butterflies to the yard with flowers. However, if you plan to use basil in your cooking, for instance, pinch the flowers off the plants as soon as you see them start to form, or else the flavor of the leaves will be affected.

- During the cold weather, keep indoor plants in a spot where they'll get as much sunlight as possible, but try to keep them away from windows and doors with drafts.

- Be sure to harvest the parts of the plants you want to use before the end of the growing season, then preserve them for use throughout the year.

- I try to steer clear of making hard-and-fast rules for gardening (or much else in life), but I'm going to strongly recommend that you don't plant mint or other mint-family herbs, such as lemon balm, in the ground with your other herbs. They will likely take over completely and soon you'll have a garden that is nothing but mint. I grow mine in large pots and cut their leaves several times a season, then dry them for later use.

Once you've got an herb garden started, there are all kinds of resources available if you need advice as you go. You can look at other books and websites, of course, but keep your eyes open for activities in your area, too. Local garden clubs abound, and most offer workshops and lectures that are free or inexpensive, like the one I attended. There is also very likely an older person in your family or neighborhood who can give you advice about growing things in the kind of soil and climate you have where you live. When it comes to gardening, no amount of reading is worth as much as experience.

Harvesting Herbs

It's a good practice to cut small harvests from your herb plants throughout the growing season. In her excellent (if old-fashioned) book *Herb Gardening in Five Seasons*, Adelma Grenier Simmons reminds us that herbs are meant to be used. Don't be shy about harvesting them. If you never cut the leaves they will end up yellowed and dead, but if you do, you'll continue to get new growth late into the fall. In fact, you may be able to get more than one harvest a season from most herb plants.

The best time of day to harvest herbs is in the morning, after the dew has dried but before all the oils have had a chance to evaporate in the sun. This way you will get the strongest, most pungent taste and aroma from your harvest. Making small cuttings from a perennial plant (most herbs are perennials) several times a season will also help it keep a fuller, rounder shape rather than getting leggy and skinny-looking.

To harvest sage, basil, thyme, and rosemary, cut the leaves. To do this, cut the whole stem rather than picking individual leaves off the plant. To harvest chives, Carey advises taking the flower before it has fully opened. To harvest fennel you want the seeds, rather than the leaves, and for horseradish, the root.

Preserving Herbs

If your herb plants grow in abundance as herbs tend to do, you will very likely end up harvesting more than you can use at once. Use one or more of these simple methods to preserve your cuttings for future use.

Make a vinegar infusion. Vinegar infused with herbs can be used in cooking, to season salads and vegetables, or in any cleaning recipe in place of plain vinegar. See *Infusions, Tinctures, and Decoctions* on page 45 for detailed instructions on making an infused vinegar.

Air drying. Air drying is the easiest way to preserve herbs and probably the loveliest too: With your kitchen festooned with bunches of drying herbs overhead, you will feel like a true kitchen witch! The reason air drying works so well is that the water in the plants will evaporate, but the essential oils won't. Dry herbs by hanging a bundle of them, tied with a string, from a hook in your ceiling or wall. Just make sure that the back of the bundle is not resting against the wall so that the whole plant dries evenly and doesn't leave marks on your wall. You can buy a special hanger that's shaped a bit like a mobile, with a circle suspended from the ceiling and several hooks arranged around the circle. You can also air dry your bundles by laying them flat on a cookie cooling rack, being sure to turn them regularly so they dry evenly. Within several days or a few weeks you'll have dried leaves or flowers that you can use however you like.

Microwave drying. This can work well, but you have to be careful not to cook the plants. We've also heard it said by credible people that if the oils in the plants get too hot, they can create a small explosion, and that sage in particular is likely to ignite. I've played around with microwave drying and haven't started any fires, but I have heard an ominous popping sound. To be safe, put just a few sprigs in at a time and check them every 30 seconds.

Dehydrator drying. You certainly don't have to run out and buy a dehydrator, but it is a very useful tool. We've had one for years because my husband likes to dry meat and fruit to eat as a snack. Ours is made up of five detachable trays that stack on top of each other, which allows the warm air to flow over and around the things being dried. You can do lots of other cool things with a dehydrator too, like drying slices of oranges to hang from string for a witchy, scented decoration.

The dehydrator will come with a booklet that explains how to dry different kinds of foods, including herb leaves, roots, and seeds. Herbs will always need to be dried at a relatively low temperature, around 90 to 100 degrees, and the drying time will vary depending on the size and type of plant. To dry a harvest of basil leaves recently, I followed the instructions and let them dry for 24 hours, checking a couple of times to be sure they weren't getting overdried. I knew the leaves were ready when one crumbled when I pinched it; if they're still pliable at all, they're not dry enough yet. Plants with smaller leaves, such as thyme, may take only a couple of hours to dry completely.

Freezing. This is an easy method and it works well. First crush the leaves with your mortar and pestle or your fingers, then put them in an ice cube tray, cover them with water, and freeze them.

If you've chosen to dry your herbs rather than freeze them and are not using them to make an infusion, you should next strip the plants and store the leaves in glass jars. Some folks recommend using only dark glass jars, but I use clear ones and store them in a dark cabinet. Stored this way, the herbs will keep well for at least a year, usually longer (though I do recommend using them before too much time has passed). I have also stored them in plastic bags, but there could be draw-backs to doing this: According to some sources, the volatile oils in the leaves can interact with the chemicals in the plastic in a way you don't want. When the plant matter has totally lost its color and scent it is no longer good to use.

Easy Household Composting

by Katie

The basic idea behind composting is that you're purposefully creating an environment where something that happens naturally—the breaking down of organic material—can be accelerated and used to your advantage. Understanding the principles behind decomposition is one thing, but there is something truly magical about composting your household waste and seeing the process for yourself. As the poet Sparrow wrote in the essay "Small Happiness," "The fact that you can take scraps of potato and cabbage, mix them with manure and grass cuttings, and create your own bountiful soil is astonishing. It's like cooking in reverse." If you're looking for an easy way to feel a deep connection to the life cycle, composting is for you.

However, I used to feel too intimidated by composting to try it. For many years I lived in apartments and thought (incorrectly, as it turned out) that I couldn't compost for that reason. Later, when I finally found myself in a house with a small backyard, I wasn't sure where to begin. I'd looked at lots of books and zines that suggested I use a plastic trash can, build a wooden frame, or stack up some old car tires to use as a structure to contain the compost, but this all seemed cumbersome and I never tried it.

When I finally took the plunge it was because I was tired of creating so much waste in the kitchen and was determined to do something about it. (Some experts estimate that half of the household waste that ends up in landfills could have been composted. Eek!) I took to YouTube and found a video of a woman making a compost pit simply by digging a hole in her yard, about 4 x 5 feet in diameter. That's exactly what I did, and I couldn't be happier with the results. Right this moment my kitchen scraps and old paperwork are busy transforming themselves into the herb plants I use to clean my home and nurture my body. To try this yourself, you'll need:

Green matter (nitrogen): fresh leaves and weeds from the garden, coffee grounds, eggshells, vegetable cuttings from the kitchen

Brown matter (carbon): dead leaves, shredded paper, wood chips, straw, manure

To begin, dig a hole in an area of your yard that gets a good amount of sun. A dark corner will stay too wet and create a stinky mess. If you don't feel like digging a hole, just start a pile on the ground. Put down a layer of green matter, add a layer of brown matter over it, and you're on your way. Every once in a while, stir the stuff in the pile to make sure it's all breaking down. After a few months of this, check the bottom of your pile: If it looks like very dark, rich soil, it's ready to be used.

I keep a take-out container or a milk carton that I've cut in half next to my sink and put my kitchen scraps in there, mostly veggie scraps leftover from cooking or pieces of houseplants I've pruned. Also in the kitchen is a paper bag full of shredded bank statements and other papers. After I've amassed a week's worth of plant "greens" I'll go out back and add them to the pile, followed by a big handful

Apartment Dwellers, Take Heart!

Happily, it is totally possible to compost even if you don't have a yard. For several years my sister composted the kitchen waste in her city apartment and used it to enrich the soil in her houseplants and her community garden plot. She recommends using a tabletop container with an activated-carbon filter to cut down on odors. Collect kitchen scraps that are left over as you cook and place them in the container. Once it's full, you can add the scraps, along with some shredded newspapers, to a compost pile in a community garden. If you don't have access to a space like this, there are many companies that will pick up your kitchen waste on a weekly basis. They'll even drop off finished compost for you to use, if you like—try adding some to the soil of your houseplants and watch those beauties flourish.

of the shredded papers or dried leaves for "browns." If the weather has been dry, I'll sprinkle some water over the whole thing too. You need a balance of greens and browns to get the composting process working right.

I compost all through the year, including the winter. As you can see I am not very exact in the way that I keep my compost but it doesn't matter; my method works great. Do what works best for you and your situation. For instance, I live in a city and don't want to attract rodents to my yard, so I don't put corn in my compost because I know rats love it.

A few other words of warning. Some manure, like cow dung, can be safely added to a compost pit, but you should never put cat poop in your compost. It contains parasites that can make you very sick if you handle it or use it in the garden. It is technically possible to compost meat and other animal products, like milk—they're organic, of course, and will break down—but it's very hard to do safely since these things can harbor bacteria and are likely to smell bad or attract animals or flies. I strongly advise against it.

To use:

Once you've got some finished compost, use it! Here in Philadelphia we have dense, clay soil that can be hard to garden, especially in a spot where the soil hasn't been turned for a long time. Last spring I dug a new bed for an herb garden and was faced with soil that looked as airtight as modeling clay, so early in the growing season I went to my compost pit in the hopes of improving it. This was about a year after starting my compost pit, and when I dug into it I met a few fat, happy earthworms, which was a great sign: Worms, along with microorganisms such as bacteria and fungi, increase the health of the soil.

All I did was sprinkle a few handfuls of compost over my garden bed in June, just after planting, and by the end of the summer my tender, baby herb plants had all grown big and lush. If you're starting a new garden you can mix the compost into the top couple of inches of soil and aerate it with a garden fork before planting. But simply sprinkling it over the top the way I did works just fine, since the nutrients from the compost will slowly be released into the soil underneath.

For a deliciously simple approach to composting, try pouring some of your used coffee grounds into the soil of your indoor potted plants now and again. My grandmother always did this and her apartment was so full of lush houseplants, it looked like a little jungle.

Citronella Mosquito Repellant

by Katie

Oh my goddess, do we get eaten alive by mosquitos in the summer. It gets muggy and buggy in this part of Pennsylvania every year, which can make it hard to sit out back or even weed the garden without getting a lot of bites. There are several different plants, and essential oils made from those plants, that have a scent that repels mosquitoes and other insects. Citronella is probably our favorite, and it's safe to apply directly to your skin. It also smells wonderful, like every summer backyard party you've ever been to.

You can make this repellant as a spray or an oil that you rub onto your skin. To make the spray, just drop citronella essential oil into grain alcohol at a ratio of one drop citronella to one milliliter (ml) grain alcohol. I filled a two-ounce spray bottle with 50 drops of citronella oil and 50 ml grain alcohol and let it solubilize for over an hour before using it. My husband, who is very delicious to mosquitoes, reported a big improvement after using this spray.

One drawback to the spray, however, is that it dissipates rather quickly and needs to be reapplied a few times an hour. Putting the essential oil into a carrier oil that you rub into your skin makes the scent last much longer. To make an oil-based balm that is safe to put on your skin, use a ratio of 10% essential oils to 90% carrier oil of your choice. Common carrier oils include coconut, olive, jojoba, or almond oil. An article published by the Tisserand Institute reports that coconut oil was shown in a peer-reviewed study to be much more effective than olive oil in this formulation, so I use coconut oil.

To make this balm, you will need:
45 milliliters coconut oil
5 milliliters citronella essential oil
Medicine measuring cup
Dark glass bottle or tin/glass jar

To make enough mosquito repellant to fill a 2-ounce bottle, simply measure out 45 milliliters of coconut oil and 5 ml of the essential oil using a medicine measuring cup, then store the combined ingredients in the glass bottle. A bottle made of dark-colored glass (blue or amber) will protect the contents more effectively than a clear glass one.

Coconut oil—the virgin, non-fractionated kind—is liquid when the temperature is higher than 76 degrees Fahrenheit, and it solidifies when it's cooler than that. You will most likely be dealing with mosquitoes when the weather is hot, but if you need it in the cooler weather, this balm can be used in its solid state as well. Store and use solid balm in a tin or, even better, a deeper glass jar, so the contents will be less likely to spill out. To apply the balm, simply scoop some up and rub it onto any exposed skin.

A preventative tip: Be sure you aren't providing a fertile breeding ground for mosquitoes by pouring out or covering any standing water near your house. They lay eggs like crazy in still water, so if you have pots, buckets, or any other containers that get filled with rainwater, turn them over when they're not in use or bring them inside.

Air Purifying Houseplants

by Katie

Houseplants have a way of making a home more vibrant and alive, kind of like auxiliary pets. They may be quieter than a cat or dog, but they're just as full of life. They also serve an important, practical purpose: They clean the air.

Plants filter the air naturally, as part of the transpiration-respiration process. They create oxygen and take in carbon dioxide, and as they do so they filter out other things that are in the air (or water). Just as animals adapt to their environment, plants do too, and some are adapted to do this better than others because of where they live. For example, plants that grow naturally in wetlands or swamplands are especially good at filtering out things from the water before putting them back into the air. People can make use of this natural phenomenon to benefit ourselves and our environment. One powerful example is phytoremediation, a process that uses photosynthesis to restore damaged soil. It's so effective that scientists, working with the government, use plants to clean the soil in poisoned wetlands and former toxic sites.

It's also possible to make use of plants' purifying properties indoors. My sister Liz is a professional horticulturist who directed me to the NASA Clean Air Study, which was conducted in the late '80s by scientists who were looking for ways to keep the air clean on space stations. They found that one plant for every 100 square feet will effectively remove certain toxins from the air, which is a good rule of thumb for all of us to use. Depending on the size of your living space, one plant per 100 square feet is approximately one plant to a room.

The plants that work best for cleaning the air inside your house are tropical plants. These are slow-growing in most parts of the United States and don't go dormant in the winter, which is what makes them good houseplants. In general, the wider the leaf and the quicker the plant grows, the more efficiently (and quickly) the plant cleans the air.

Here are some of Liz's favorite air purifying houseplants:

- Snake plant (*Sansevieria trifasciata*), also called mother-in-law's tongue. This is one of the most common plants used for air purification. It works well because it has wide leaves.

- Spider plant (*Chlorophytum elatum*). This is easy to grow and has lots of little pups that can be removed and put into their own pots to grow.

- Dracaena. This looks like a palm, with a lot of narrow leaves. One common variety has a red edge.

- Ficus. Native to Asia and Australia, these are very common as houseplants and are easy to grow (i.e., hard to kill).

- Pothos (*Epipremnum aureum*). Pothos has lots of common names, including devil's ivy and money plant. This plant grows incredibly long tendrils and is very easy to keep alive.

- Philodendron. There are a great many types of philodendrons, and many of them have large leaves. Elephant ear (*Philodendron domesticum*) is a common ornamental garden plant but it can be grown inside too, and it looks really cool. Start one as a bulb in a container.

- Aloe. These beautiful succulents filter benzene, a known carcinogen that comes from both natural and industrial sources, including some glues, paints, commercial furniture wax, and detergents.

If you are strategically putting houseplants in your home for the purpose of cleaning the air, be sure to wash and repot them every six months to a year, since the nasties they've drawn from the air will then just be sitting in the soil. And while it might sound silly to say, don't eat any part of the plants or the soil they're in.

Into the Wild: A Note on Foraging

by Katie

Foraging, sometimes called wildcrafting, means harvesting berries, leaves, nuts, and other plant life that are growing wild. And of course people have been doing it for centuries to gather plants for both food and medicine. It's what I did when I gathered berries that were growing by the river to use in a fabric dyeing project. But couldn't taking plants from where they're growing be unethical or harmful to do? It's a complicated area and not everyone agrees, but foraging can be environmentally friendly and even helpful when it's done the right way.

Advocates of wildcrafting, such as the Association of Foragers, believe that if it's done responsibly and knowledgeably it is not only safe, but beneficial to plants, people, and our shared habitats. By practicing "bioregional herbalism," you'll use fewer resources in the form of transporting the herbs from a faraway place to a store close to where you live. At the same time, the famous herbalist Rosemary Gladstar warns that some wildflowers and herbs are being endangered by overcollection—especially as herbalism becomes a commercial enterprise for an increasing number of people.

When considering taking a cutting from any plant that is growing in the wild, you should first be able to identify the plant and understand its growth cycle. For one thing, you could be putting yourself at risk if you accidentally take a cutting from a plant that gives you an allergic reaction. It's also important not to overharvest. Only take as much as you can use quickly, and never take more than 10 percent of a plant. Don't touch the strongest, fullest plants in a stand at all.

You can help native plant populations by harvesting invasive species, which can overtake large areas and disrupt local ecosystems. In their book *Healing Appalachia: Sustainable Living through Appropriate Technology*, Al Fritsch and Paul Gallimore tell us we can help ourselves to wild-growing blackberries, blueberries, and elderberries without doing any damage to the larger supply, but remind us to knock down old briars and leave the younger, green ones alone since they'll bear fruit the following year.

Also remember that in the U.S. there are federal, state, and local foraging laws to keep in mind—you can't just go picking any old where! Wildcrafting can be fun and rewarding, but we advise you to read and think carefully before trying it yourself.

Creating a Backyard Wildlife Sanctuary

by Nadine

A garden is the mirror of a mind.

–Henry Beston, *Herbs and the Earth*

A t the heart of kitchen witchery is the idea that humans and nature are so deeply connected that one can help to heal the other. Nature has provided us with life, and in return, we can use our powers to take care of the plants and animals around our homes.

The house I live in, one of many in a neighborhood that resembles the set of a 1950s TV show, sits on a half-acre lot that offers refuge for all the creatures that call this area home. My human neighbors prefer bright green lawns, uniform hedges, and the common varieties of ornamental flowers. This orderly, conventional aesthetic is not incompatible with wildlife, but landscaping created specifically for animals can do so much more. No matter how small your yard, it too can become a wildlife sanctuary.

To get started on making your yard more appealing to your non-human neighbors, first plant some native vegetation. That is, the flowers, trees, and shrubs that used to grow there before your neighborhood existed. Many of the flowers can be started from seed, and your local nursery may carry native young plants as well as shrubs and trees. To maximize the available yard space, select plants that can do more than one task. For example, flowering trees and shrubs that produce fruits, seeds, or nuts will feed pollinators, birds, and mammals while also providing shelter and nesting material for those same creatures. If you already have an herb garden (pollinators do love those European herbs) just add in a few native flowers. You may notice some interesting new insects joining the garden party.

Native plants vary by region, of course. A quick internet search will reveal what plants call your area home. For reference, I've had success with the following plants around my house in Pennsylvania, and they all should do well in the northeast quadrant of the United States. The garden beds at one point or another have held: purple coneflower (*Echinacea purpurea*), ox eye sunflower (*Heliopsis helianthoides*), lavender hyssop (*Agastache foeniculum*), wild bergamot (*Monarda fistulosa*), purple horsemint or lemon balm (*Monarda citriodora*), and cardinal flower (*Lobelia cardinalis*). Two elderberry bushes (*Sambucus canadensis*) grow by the fence in the backyard. Pokeweed, disliked by many homeowners as it can spread rather aggressively, pops up everywhere the birds drop its seeds. I allow a handful to reach their full size in a few select spots around the yard. All parts of this plant are toxic to most mammals, including humans, who also risk getting an itchy rash if it touches their skin. However, birds, especially those that migrate through the area, expect to find the dark purple berries it produces late in the summer.

Next, let's turn to the largest part of a standard yard: the lawn. The ideal American lawn is short, dense, and even, just like a golf course. If this is your lawn, consider allowing so-called weeds to grow among the grass. Many of these plants are not natives, but they are not invasive and do offer some benefits. For example, dandelions are one of the first flowers to bloom in spring and therefore provide much needed food for early insects. On my front lawn they create a cheerful carpet of yellow blooms that shouts *Happy Spring!* at everyone walking by. Another helpful non-native is white Dutch clover. This is an ideal lawn plant because it doesn't grow very tall and it produces tons of flowers, which pollinators and rabbits appear to enjoy very much. I sprinkle clover seeds over every bald spot on my lawn, and the clover endures much better than the grass it replaces.

Besides native plants, the next most important thing wildlife needs is water. Birds love a birdbath, but squirrels and even some insects also appreciate fresh water. You can buy a stone or concrete birdbath basin, with or without a matching pedestal, or make your own with things

Spider Web Visualization

by Nadine

Near the end of summer spiders spin their webs all over the hedges around my house. Covered in dew or raindrops, the silky threads throw off rainbow shimmers in the sun. One October a very large spider made a very large web on the back porch, right next to the door. Walking up to the door on a blustery night I noticed that at a certain angle I could see the spider perfectly, a black silhouette against the light streaming out from the kitchen window, but if I moved just a tiny bit, the spider and its web disappeared. Thank goodness I know this spider is here, I thought, or else I would panic seeing it suddenly leap out of the darkness right at my face. It occurred to me then that a spider would make a very good home guardian, scaring away anyone who would attempt to break in.

So now whenever I feel anxious about leaving my house unattended when my boyfriend and I go on vacation, or if I hear a strange noise while I'm home alone at night, I summon the spiders in a visualization exercise. First, I imagine them in the hedges weaving their webs, and then as the webs grow they extend out to touch the walls of the house, soon covering the doors and windows, then reaching over the roof. Eventually all of the webs knit together, shrouding the whole house in one huge shimmery cocoon. My home is now safe.

you already have around the house. For example, I placed a Pyrex glass pie plate directly on the ground under a hedge. Right up under the lip of the plate I tucked a flat paving stone to act as a sort of ramp to help animals get in and out. In the center of the plate I put a teacup saucer, upside down, that sticks partly out of the water. Creating a kind of island like this gives birds a dry area to stand on and also enables them to judge the depth of the water. Another household object that makes a wonderful birdbath is a terracotta flower pot saucer. I replaced a broken concrete basin with an extra-large saucer that fits perfectly on the old basin's pedestal, and used a smaller terracotta saucer as the center island.

Give your birdbath a good rinse daily (in summer I do it twice a day) and refill it with fresh water. Be sure not to put in more than about one inch of water, and do not allow rainwater to accumulate. Birds, especially fledglings, can drown in relatively shallow depths if their wings get too wet. If you use a garden hose to fill the birdbath, make sure that hose does not contain lead. At the height of summer a birdbath quickly collects dirt, leaves, feathers, seed shells, and, unfortunately, bird poo. Clean the birdbath once a week or as soon as it starts looking grungy, because it can breed and spread disease. Concrete basins and terracotta saucers can be cleaned with a mixture of vinegar and baking soda scrubbed around with an old toothbrush. If algae, which grows rapidly, has already settled in, use a very mild bleach solution instead. Rinse the birdbath thoroughly before refilling it.

While native plants can feed wildlife all on their own, depending on your particular backyard offerings you may want to provide some supplemental food in a bird feeder. Please note that if your home is in an urban area or surrounded by woods, a bird feeder could attract animals that you would rather not invite into your yard, such as rats and bears, respectively. I prefer feeders made of a combination of glass and metal, not plastic. Clean the feeder at least every two weeks with dish soap. Every few cleanings I will also use a very mild bleach solution. Just like birdbaths, feeders can breed and spread disease. Place the feeder near trees or shrubs to ensure that birds feel safe during their visit. Different birds prefer different kinds of seeds, so research what the birds in your area would like. Squirrels, of course, are not very picky. If they tend to hog the feeder, give them their own stash elsewhere to distract them, at least for a little while. I leave little piles around the maple tree they live in, and then some more all around the edge of the yard for the rabbits.

Finally, if we want to provide a home for all living things then we must learn to see the beauty of plants throughout their entire lifecycle. The common practice of removing all of a garden's dead plant material at the end of the growing season may enhance your property's curb appeal, but it does nothing to support the health of its ecosystem. The work of a garden continues even after the flowers have finished blooming, so just let it be. In late summer and into the fall, migrating birds may depend on the seeds offered up by dried flower stalks to help them continue on their long journey, and spiders drape spooky webs between the brown and black stems to catch the last insects of the season. Dried leaves on the ground nourish the soil as they decompose. Dropped flower heads release their seeds over winter and so plant next year's garden for you. To the untrained human eye a garden without greenery looks like death, but death is not only the end of life, it is the beginning of life as well.

As the human entrusted with the care of your little plot of the Earth you may feel a profound sense of responsibility to keep it happy and healthy. I certainly do. But remember, nothing in nature is one-sided. On one stressful spring morning I left the house in a frazzled daze. The day's to-list played on a continuous loop in my mind as I completed my daily routine—check feeders, change birdbath water—on autopilot. Yet, instead of immediately returning to the house as usual, I found myself crouched down next to the borage, mesmerized by the bumblebees zipping around the blue, star-shaped flowers as sunlight embraced me in a warm hug. The crushing weight of stress I had lugged around all morning lifted and a cool breeze carried it away. It turns out that my backyard had created a sanctuary for me, too.

Holistic
Self-Care

Introduction

Years later a series of events reintroduced me to DIY skincare. It began when my favorite cleansing balm got discontinued. I desperately searched for a replacement, but could find nothing comparable. Next, I came across a YouTube video that showed how to use olive oil to remove makeup. This worked beautifully, and I remembered that coconut oil was an ingredient in that balm. Then one afternoon while walking around Reading Terminal Market in Philadelphia I noticed tubs of shea butter on display at the herb shop. Realizing that the main ingredients of that balm were sold right there in the market I knew I could try to make it myself.

After several attempts, I made a balm that was not quite like the one that had inspired my experiment, but it worked just as well. I felt like an alchemist who had finally transformed lead into gold. Suddenly, all my skincare products looked different. The magic of branding— pretty packaging, alluring fragrances—had convinced me that these products each contained a unique essence, while in reality many of them were made of the same basic ingredients. The spell was broken. I now had a little glass jar filled with a beautiful balm and an empowering new perspective.

This section of the book is dedicated to caring for the body and the mind using the principles and methods of kitchen witchery. In the following pages you will learn how to: work with natural ingredients to care for skin and hair, incorporate aromatherapy into daily routines, and use a few tools from the practice of Witchcraft to support your mental wellbeing. While experimenting and creating you will also learn about yourself, what you enjoy and what you are capable of. Through the magic of kitchen witchery you may discover that the most powerful thing you could ever brew up in your kitchen is a belief in yourself.

Safety Precautions

Please consult your dermatologist if you are currently being treated for a skin condition before you begin experimenting with skincare ingredients. Similarly, if you have a specific skin concern, consult a dermatologist to get their professional advice. The suggestions and recipes in this book are not meant to

The Magic Ingredient

Although the word "magic" never appears on product ingredient lists despite what ads may suggest, we have the power to imbue our own creations with intentions and use them as part of our daily routines, thus transforming them into rituals. For example, a makeup remover infused with the idea of self-acceptance might contain essential oils of rose or ylang ylang, two flowers associated with love. In the evening, as we wipe off the day's mask of makeup, this balm reminds us that our natural face is beautiful and that we deserve respect and love. Similarly, applying a lip balm, perhaps tinted red (the color of courage), and created for self-expression, reminds us to speak up and assert ourselves. Whatever our personal struggles, we can create products to soothe and heal more than our skin and hair.

treat any serious skin condition. I have absolutely no professional qualifications in this area whatsoever.

Avoid any ingredients if you know or even just suspect you are allergic to them. If using an ingredient for the first time, do a patch test first. Apply a small amount of the ingredient to your inner arm, cover it with a bandaid, and wait 48 hours. If a rash has appeared, do not use that ingredient.

Also, everyone is different. We have different skin and hair types and what works for one person may not work for someone else. Our genetic makeup, medications we take, the water quality in our homes, and our local climate all play a role in how ingredients affect us.

Remedies For Skin And Hair

Before you begin experimenting, go back to Section 1 of this book and familiarize yourself with important details on ingredients and equipment, tips for preparing containers, and instructions for the techniques referenced in some recipes. A few recipes call for the use of a washcloth. Katie teaches you how to make your own in *Knit a Dishcloth* on page 80.

Steam

Steam has been used since the time of Roman bathhouses as part of a complete skincare ritual. It softens and dampens skin, and its warmth increases blood circulation. This may make skin more receptive to subsequent treatments like exfoliation and masks.

To create a basic facial steam, pour boiling water into a heatproof bowl (a small mixing bowl works well) and carefully lower your face into the steam. To prolong the experience, cover your head and the bowl with a towel to prevent the steam from evaporating away too quickly.

For an aromatic, spa-like experience, place dried herbs, such as lavender flowers, into the bowl and then add the boiling water.

For added skin benefits, try essential oils. I've found that using very hot, steaming but not yet boiling water keeps the scent of the essential oils going longer. Pour the water into a bowl, then add in two or three drops of essential oil. Tea tree and lavender are traditional choices to fight acne, while frankincense is believed to support aging skin.

Aroma Fizzlers

Baths, with all their fancy additives like herbs, oils, salts, and fizzy bombs, are an indulgent pastime for some, but not everyone has a bathtub, or the patience to enjoy a good long soak. Being in the latter category, I still sometimes want to bring a bit of bathtub pizzazz to my shower. An aroma fizzler does the trick by adding a scent and an entertaining fizzle.

Ingredients:
1/2 cup baking soda
1/4 cup citric acid
Water
Essential oils
Yield: ¾ cup or 3 fizzlers

In a bowl, stir the baking soda and citric acid together. To this you need to add water, but only the tiniest amount. This is best achieved by using a spray bottle that creates a fine mist, but adding one to two drops of water directly to the mixture will also work. Stir everything together, including a generous amount of essential oils. Do not add more water until you have thoroughly combined everything and tested the consistency. The mixture should only just stick together when squeezed in your hand. If you have any cuts on your hands, wear rubber gloves when touching the mixture. Citric acid stings like crazy.

Some scent suggestions: grapefruit to wake you up, lavender for relaxation, eucalyptus to ease congestion, peppermint for general wellbeing.

Next, you will need three ¼ cup molds. A standard-sized metal muffin pan or paper cupcake wrappers work well. Press the mixture firmly into the moldsor form the mixture into three pucks, 1/4 cup each, by hand. Set the hand-formed fizzlers on a non-porous surface, like a plate. Allow the fizzlers to dry completely, which could take a few hours. To release the fizzlers from a metal muffin pan, turn it upside and tap it on the counter. If your finished fizzlers don't smell as strong as you'd like, add more essential oil on top and let that soak in before using them. Store the fizzlers in a glass jar.

To use a fizzler in the shower, place it in an area where it will get a little bit wet, but well away from the direct stream of the shower. Water activates the fizzing, which releases the scent. Too much water all at once will dissolve the fizzler before the scent has time to evaporate. Please note that a dissolving fizzler can make the shower floor slippery.

Variation: To make a moisturizing aroma fizzler for a bath (i.e., a bath bomb) add one tablespoon of oil and/or melted cocoa butter or shea butter to the citric acid and baking soda mixture, and then add the water. If using essential oils, drop them into the oil or melted butter before mixing with the dry ingredients.

Herbal Rinses

Hot water infusions of herbs, commonly called herbal teas or tisanes (or simply tea if made from the leaves of the tea plant), can be used to care for skin and hair. While scientists have studied some herbs, much of what is known about them appears to come from folk medicine and centuries of anecdotal evidence. I recommend reading product ingredient lists as well as herbals to help you choose an herb that could work for you. For example, try calendula if your favorite moisturizer features it as its star ingredient. Some other herbs that appear in skincare products are chamomile, green tea, lady's mantle, lavender, licorice root, and marshmallow root. Common shampoo ingredients include hops, rosemary, and chamomile, which are believed to add volume, support hair growth, and bring out blond tones, respectively.

To make an herbal tea to use as a rinse, prepare a hot water infusion using about one tablespoon of herbs per cup of distilled water. Let it steep, covered, at least 20 minutes. Store leftovers in the fridge and use them within a day or two.

To use an herbal tea as skincare, apply it to clean skin with a cotton pad or put it in a spray bottle and spritz it on. Alternatively, use it in a clay mask or herbal scrub. For a full body herbal experience, place a drawstring muslin bag or a large tea ball filled with herbs into your bath water. A couple tea bags will work as well. Or just pour the strained infusion directly into the bath.

To use an herbal tea on hair, first shampoo and rinse your hair and then apply the herbal tea. Pour it directly onto your hair or spritz it on with a spray bottle. Then either rinse it out or not, whichever you prefer.

Clove Mouthwash

Cloves contain an anesthetic property, which is why they are an old remedy for treating tooth pain. Try it for yourself by gently biting down on a whole clove with your back teeth. Hold it there for a while and eventually that entire area of your mouth will feel like it was injected with a teeny tiny bit of Novocain. Though not a pain-reliever, a mouthwash made from cloves, which may contain antibacterial properties, freshens the breath and makes teeth feel clean.

To make the mouthwash, prepare a hot water infusion using distilled water. Use about one tablespoon of cloves per cup of water. Let it steep, covered, for about 30 minutes. Pour the infusion into a clean glass jar or bottle, straining out the cloves. Store the mouthwash in the fridge and keep it for no more than six months. Discard the liquid if it starts to look cloudy.

To use, mix about half a teaspoon of the clove infusion with about one tablespoon of warm water. Swish it around your mouth just like you would any other mouthwash. Do not swallow. To help heal any kind of cut or sore in your mouth, add a sprinkle of salt to the warm water.

Herbal Face Scrub

In this mild face scrub, powdered herbs gently exfoliate while oats provide a slippery froth when mixed with water. These ingredients create a calming scent that makes the scrub quite pleasant to use before bed. See *Herbal Rinses* for a list of other herbs that could work in this recipe.

Ingredients:
1 teaspoon rolled oats
1 teaspoon dried chamomile
1 teaspoon dried lavender flowers
½ teaspoon cosmetic clay (optional)
Yield: 3 to 3 ½ teaspoons

Crush all ingredients, except the clay, with a mortar and pestle. It doesn't need to be perfectly powdery or uniform. Then stir in the clay, if using. Store the scrub in a tin or small glass jar.

To use, mix a small amount of the scrub with either plain water, a hydrosol, an herbal tea, or witch hazel water to form a wet paste and spread it over dampened skin. Rub the scrub around in circular motions, then rinse off with warm water. If the scrub contains clay, leave the paste on for a few minutes like a mask.

Witch Hazel Water

Witch hazel is a distilled extract made from the bark of the North American witch hazel tree. It is astringent, meaning it causes soft tissues to contract together, a property that is helpful for healing minor skin injuries like cuts, burns, and bruises. Commercial witch hazel products called witch hazel astringents contain skin-safe alcohol and products called witch hazel toners, which may or may not contain alcohol, and could include ingredients like aloe vera, rosewater, glycerin, and preservatives, among others.

Witch hazel astringents and toners are simple, effective skincare products. Used after cleansing the skin, they remove any leftover residues of soap, sunscreen, and makeup. They deep-clean the pores, which can make them appear smaller, and they reduce inflammation and redness. Witch hazel astringent, because it contains alcohol, can help to balance oily skin. Alcohol-free toner is recommended for skin that is sensitive or dry.

For years I have used witch hazel astringent as a toner. When I saw that my local herb shop carries dried witch hazel bark I decided to find out what a simple preparation of witch hazel bark and water would do to my skin. To help ensure that the bark's beneficial properties were released into the water I made a decoction rather than a hot water infusion. Decoctions are the recommended method for preparing woody material like bark.

I applied this witch hazel water every morning and evening after washing my face, which is how I normally use witch hazel astringent. After doing this for a week, my skin looked and felt fine . Yet, something was a little different, and I assume it had to do with the lack of alcohol in the witch hazel water. Whenever I have used alcohol-free witch hazel toners my skin has had a similar reaction. A few days into the following week the liquid became cloudy, a sign that it was turning. Had I kept it refrigerated it would have lasted at least another week.

In conclusion, this experiment taught me that while I prefer witch hazel astringent, a witch hazel decoction makes a good substitute if needed. People who prefer alcohol-free toners might find that witch hazel water works just as well. Besides using it as a toner, witch hazel water can be mixed with an herbal scrub or combined with clay to make a mask.

Wicked Witch Face Mask

Every once in a while my skin seems to require a really thorough cleaning. The most efficient method to accomplish this is with an intensive clay mask. I recommend doing this mask at night so that your skin can recover while you sleep.

Ingredients:

French green clay

Witch hazel astringent

Place approximately one tablespoon, maybe a little bit less, of French green clay into a small bowl. Add witch hazel just a few drops at a time while stirring the mixture. If you add too much witch hazel just put in a bit more clay, and vice versa. The ideal consistency resembles thick, wet mud.

Spread the mixture over clean, slightly damp skin, staying well clear of the eyes and the thin skin of the under-eye area. As the mask dries your face will sort of throb. Do not be alarmed! The clay brings blood to the surface of the skin and it should, in theory, be drawing dirt and oil out of the pores at the same time. Once the mask has dried, press a washcloth soaked with warm water over your face to soften up the now very cracked and hardened clay, and then use the washcloth to gently remove it. Since this mask basically acts like an extremely potent toner, it's a good idea to follow up with a gentle moisturizer and end your nighttime skincare routine right there.

For more sensitive skin, replace the witch hazel astringent with an alcohol-free witch hazel toner, or the witch hazel water from the previous recipe. Or eliminate the witch hazel entirely and use a hydrosol or herbal tea. For a more exfoliating effect, try a bit of raw apple cider vinegar mixed with water.

To help heal a breakout, try salt water. Add just a pinch of unrefined salt like Dead Sea salt or Himalayan salt to some warm water in order to dissolve it and then mix that with the clay. This mask may sting a bit as it dries. Once it's washed off, apply a soothing moisturizer.

Other kinds of clay like kaolin (sometimes called white cosmetic or china clay) or bentonite can be used instead of French green. All cosmetic clays extract impurities and oil from skin, but the French green variety is more absorbent than others and increases blood circulation, making it extremely effective at deep cleaning and toning.

Of course you don't have to put a mask over your entire face. If there's just one little problem area, apply the mask like a spot treatment.

Apple Cider Vinegar

Apple cider vinegar (ACV), made from fermented apples, contains malic acid, which is an alpha hydroxy acid that acts as a chemical exfoliant. I prefer to use raw ACV on skin just in case all those bacteria it contains are beneficial, but the filtered, inexpensive ACV is good enough for hair.

To use ACV as an exfoliating toner, dilute it with water by about half and apply it to the face or another part of the body with a cotton pad. If your skin is not used to chemical exfoliants, you may want to dilute it even more. Please note that the toner could sting and your skin might turn red temporarily. This is normal. If you have a stronger reaction than this, discontinue using ACV on your skin. Freshly exfoliated skin is more susceptible to sun damage, so be sure to apply sunscreen on any areas you used the toner for at least a couple days following application.

For hair, try apple cider vinegar as a rinse. Not only does it remove built up residue from products and hard water, it makes hair soft and shiny. After washing out your shampoo, apply the apple cider vinegar, and then rinse it out with water. Use a spray bottle or pour it over your hair using a container with a narrow opening like a shampoo bottle. Take care not to get it in your eyes. .You can use ACV straight to remove a lot of build up, or diluted with water if you want to use it regularly.

In general, you only want to rinse your hair, not your scalp. Applying ACV to the scalp on a regular basis can over-exfoliate the skin. However, if you have an itchy scalp, adding a few drops of tea tree essential oil to the ACV can really help, as Katie discovered. After shampooing and rinsing, spray the tea tree oil and ACV mixture on your scalp, then rinse it off. Be sure to keep your head protected from the sun for a couple days.

Aloe Vera

My paternal grandmother always kept aloe vera plants in her home to use as a first-aid remedy, and they probably lost quite a few leaves when her six children were young. Aloe is an easy-going houseplant that grows quickly, can purify indoor air, and gives its healing potion generously. The clear gel in the leaves is antimicrobial and acts as a humectant, and so helps to keep a wound clean and moisturized as it heals, which can minimize scarring. It is no wonder that aloe vera gel is the key ingredient in all those commercial products that soothe sunburned skin.

To obtain gel from the plant, simply break off a leaf and squeeze out the clear liquid. Store the leaf in the fridge and use the gel within a couple days. Probably the best way to use fresh aloe in skincare is as an occasional spot treatment. This could help soothe certain kinds of acne as well as very dry patches of skin.

If you want to use aloe on a regular basis, commercially produced aloe vera gel with minimal added ingredients works well as a substitute and will give your plant a break. Use it as a face mask (wash it off after five minutes or just let it fully absorb), or try mixing it with a bit of your everyday products like a shower gel, lotion, or shampoo to give them additional moisturizing properties.

Victorian Rose Skin Softener

Have you ever wondered why we tend to call floral fragrances, especially rose, "old lady" or "grandmother" scents? Beverly Plummer, in her 1975 book *Fragrance: How to Make Natural Soaps, Scents, and Sundries*, attributes a recipe for a glycerine and rosewater skin softener treatment to her grandmother, and she describes the scent as old-fashioned. Reading this for the first time, I wondered if I had solved the mystery. Perhaps it was the women of Plummer's grandmother's generation, presumably born in the late 19th century, who doused themselves in rosewater, and this is the scent that lingers in our collective memory? I'm afraid we'll never know the true origin of "eau de grandmother," but maybe if we all start smelling of rosewater we'll bring it back in style. If rose really isn't the scent for you, maybe try another Victorian favorite like lavender or orange blossom.

Ingredients:
Vegetable glycerine
Rose hydrosol

To use this as a quick hand treatment, apply a couple sprays or drops of hydrosol onto your hands, then add a drop or two of vegetable glycerine. Rub the ingredients together and all over your hands. They may feel a bit sticky before the solution absorbs. Once it does, your hands will feel incredibly smooth and soft.

To use the softener on larger areas of the body, place the two ingredients, in whatever quantity works for you, in a glass jar or bottle. Shake the container to mix up the product before using it. To give it even more healing properties, add some aloe vera gel (from a bottle or straight from the plant). Store it in the fridge to keep it fresh for as long as possible. Throw it away if it starts to look or smell weird.

Cucumber

The humble cucumber has been usedby humans for its cooling and soothing properties for centuries. Nicholas Culpeper, the eminent 17th century herbalist, recommended cucumber juice as a remedy for watery eyes and to soothe skin suffering from sunburn and inflammation. Today cucumber extract appears in many eye creams that claim to depuff, brighten, and hydrate. While skincare products may or may not work as advertised, a cucumber can always be trusted to treat the delicate skin around the eyes with care.

To make a soothing eye mask, place thin slices of cucumber over your closed eyes and let them sit for at least 10 minutes. This will reduce puffiness, freshen the skin, and temporarily relieve itching caused by hay fever. Pair this with a facemask to complete the home spa experience.

Alternatively, saturate either two cotton pads or a washcloth with cold water. Squeeze out the excess and then add a few drops or spritzes of cucumber hydrosol.

Honey

Raw honey has been used to heal skin for thousands of years. It is a humectant, which means it draws moisture to itself, and it is antibacterial. A mask made from raw honey can benefit pretty much any skin type, from acne-prone to very dry. Simply spread it over the face (or other troubled area) and leave it on for about 10 minutes. Remove it with warm water and a washcloth.

Oats

Oats are a traditional remedy for dry, itchy skin. The oat (*Avena sativa*) contains saponins, which froth when mixed with water, and mucilage, which gives oatmeal its characteristic gelatinous texture. For best results, use rolled oats in skincare preparations.

To make a mask for the face or anywhere on the body, like dry winter hands, cook the oats just as you would to prepare oatmeal. You can use water or any kind of milk you prefer. Spread the cooled oatmeal over the skin and let it sit for about 10 minutes. Rinse it off with warm water. Store leftovers in the fridge and use them within a day or two. To revive older oatmeal and make it spreadable, add a bit of warm water.

To get a full body oat treatment, put oats into a drawstring muslin bag or a large tea ball and drop it into your bathwater. To use oats in the shower, gently scrub a drawstring muslin bag filled with oats over wet skin.

Lemon + Sun Hair Lightener

To amplify the natural bleaching effect that sunlight has on hair in the summer, all you need is lemon juice, directly from the fruit or out of a bottle. Katie and I both learned this trick from our mothers when we were kids.

To create streaks of highlights, saturate a cotton ball with the juice and then run it over a small section of hair. Or put the lemon juice into a spray bottle and spritz it all over. Do not get lemon juice on your scalp or any other areas of your skin (it can burn severely in the sun) or on clothing (it can bleach fabric). After applying the juice, wash your hands thoroughly. Then go outside to a bright spot (wearing sunscreen, of course) and let the sun work its magic.

Salt and Sugar Scrubs

Large sugar crystals and salts made of hard, coarse grains (i.e., sea salt, Himalayan, kosher) make very effective body scrubs. The particles are rough but not sharp, providing a gentle physical exfoliation. Sugar contains glycolic acid, an alpha hydroxy acid, so it exfoliates chemically as well. Salt can help heal irritated or broken skin, so it's a good choice to use on areas like the legs that have suffered small cuts and razor burn.

To make a body scrub, mix the sugar or salt with either an oil or a liquid castile soap. Add just enough oil or soap to bring the crystals or grains together so that the mixture can spread easily over the skin without being runny. To use, wet your skin in the shower, then turn off the water. Apply the scrub with your hands using circular motions. Turn the water back on and wash off the scrub. Please note that oil can make the tub or shower floor slippery.

Sugar also works as a lip scrub. Use a fine white sugar or crush up larger sugar crystals with a mortar and pestle. For one application you will not need more than just a pinch of sugar. To make the sugar spreadable, mix it with a drop of oil or honey. Apply the scrub with your finger and rub it around gently in circular motions. Remove the scrub with a damp washcloth, then apply a lip balm. To protect your freshly exfoliated lips from the sun use a lip balm that contains sunscreen.

Makeup Remover Oil

The easiest and most efficient way to remove makeup is with just an oil: extra virgin olive, unrefined coconut, avocado, and hemp seed all work very well, as they are heavy culinary oils. Skincare oils such as sweet almond, jojoba, and grapeseed also get the job done.

Your skin may respond positively or negatively to certain oils. For example, some people find that coconut oil causes breakouts. My skin has never had a bad reaction to any oil I've tried, but for some reason avocado gives it a smoother, healthier appearance. Of course, avoid any oil if you are allergic to the plant from which it's made.

Oil is attracted to oil, so the cleaning oil removes makeup, sunscreen, and excess skin oil (called sebum), but does not strip the skin of moisture. Because jojoba oil is similar to sebum, it is commonly recommended for oily and acne-prone skin.

To use oil as a makeup remover, just pour a bit onto a cotton pad or into your hands, and rub it gently all over your face in circular motions. Stubborn mascara and eyeliner come off more easily when you hold a cotton pad over your closed eyes to let the oil really soak in. As an added benefit, this conditions your lashes and over time they may grow longer and thicker.

Remove the oil with warm water and a washcloth. Then wash with your regular facial cleanser to take off any remaining residue, which, if left on, could lead to breakouts.

Oil for the Face and Body

An oil can be used all by itself as a moisturizer on the face and body. I prefer oils specifically made to be used as skincare, because culinary oils tend to feel quite heavy and uncomfortable, and they are more likely to cause breakouts. However, people with very dry skin may find culinary oils work better for them.

To give the oil aromatherapeutic and potential skincare benefits, add in some essential oils. Decant a small amount of oil into a separate glass bottle or jar and then add a few drops of essential oil.

Dried herbs, like the ones listed in *Herbal Rinses*, can be infused into oils to provide potential skincare benefits as well. See *Oil Infusions* on page 47.

Olive Oil Hair Glosser

Many shampoos and conditioners promote the nourishing oils they contain to make hair smooth and shiny. An oil treatment can do something similar, and extra virgin olive oil works beautifully.

Begin by brushing your dry hair and parting it as you normally do. Then apply the oil with your hands, avoiding your scalp. A little bit of oil goes very far, so start with less as you can always add more. Your hair does not need to be saturated.. Let it sit for at least five minutes, then shampoo and rinse your hair thoroughly. Now, you could stop there or do a rinse with apple cider vinegar. Rinsing with ACV will remove more oil from your hair, making it less likely to still look oily once it has dried. However, it may reduce the strength of the shine. Either way, do not use conditioner. Please note that oil will make the tub or shower floor slippery.

Once your hair has dried it might still look oily, possibly even if you rinsed with ACV. For this reason it's a good idea to do this treatment when you may not care too much about how your hair looks for a day, or however long you wait before washing it again. After the second shampooing your hair should be superbly glossy. This effect could last through several more washes.

Romantic Lip and Cheek Tint

Here's a recipe, modified for modern use, courtesy of an 18th century guide, *The Toilet of Flora*, not unlike the one you're reading now. Labelled simply "238. A Rouge for the Face," it is one of several recipes for cheek tints in a section titled "Carmines." It creates a glowing flush suitable for the person wishing to achieve a more natural look in line with the aesthetics of the Romantic era. Think Marie Antoinette wearing a white chemise dress galavanting around the gardens at Le Petit Trianon, not the Queen of France in a towering hairdo greeting guests at a palace ball. This red tint is *subtle*.

Ingredients:
1 tablespoon alkanet root, dried
Skincare oil (enough to cover the alkanet root)
Witch hazel astringent or vodka/grain alcohol
Yield: approximately 1 tablespoon

Infuse the alkanet root in the oil following the instructions for *Oil Infusions* on page 47. I chose to use sweet almond oil, because "oil of almonds" is mentioned frequently in *The Toilet of Flora*. It is also a relatively lightweight and comfortable skincare oil.

To use, pour a bit of witch hazel astringent or vodka/grain alcohol onto a cotton pad. Pour a bit of the tinted oil onto a clean surface, like a plate or bowl, and then dip the cotton pad into the tinted oil. Dab this onto cheeks and lips as desired. The stain should last for a few hours.

Since this is an oil-based product, it gives cheeks a pretty glow, but the oil never quite absorbs or dries down completely. Setting it with translucent powder mattifies it a bit. On the lips, a balm on top of the tint counteracts the drying effect of the witch hazel astringent or alcohol and helps the color stay on longer. The tinted oil can be incorporated into a lip balm recipe.

Butters: Shea and Cocoa

Two common butters found in skincare products are shea and cocoa. Just like oils, they can be mixed into balms or used alone as moisturizers. Shea butter is quite thick and therefore works best on small areas. Cocoa butter is hard and brittle at room temperature, but once it touches the skin it melts rapidly and spreads easily. The effect is similar to using an oil.

Scented (or not) Powder

This simple powder is probably not powerful enough to replace your deodorant, but it does absorb moisture and makes skin feel smooth and soft.

Ingredients:

½ cup arrowroot powder or cornstarch

¼ cup cosmetic clay

Essential oils (optional)

Yield: ¾ cup

In a bowl, whisk together the powder and clay, then transfer the mixture to a container. A spice jar with a sifter is ideal since you can better control how much comes out, but any small jar works just fine. Drop in the essential oils, if using, adjusting the amount to get the desired intensity of scent. Close the lid and shake vigorously to incorporate the essential oil into the powder and clay.

Baking soda is often found in natural deodorants because it absorbs odor as well as moisture, but it can irritate the skin and cause itching. If you want to use baking soda, try substituting it for half of the arrowroot/cornstarch.

Deodorant Cream

After two failed attempts of trying to copy my favorite natural deodorant—one was too oily, the other too waxy—I paused to really think about what a deodorant cream needs in order to work: a powder to absorb moisture and a vehicle like a soft balm that spreads easily and absorbs into the skin without leaving an oily residue. Here is what I came up with.

Ingredients:

1 tablespoon shea butter

3 tablespoons arrowroot powder or cornstarch

1/8th teaspoon sweet almond oil (or other skincare oil)

10 drops of essential oil (optional)

Yield: approximately 4 tablespoons or 2 ounces

Melt the shea butter in the top of a double boiler. Stir in the arrowroot powder or cornstarch and the oil, then add the essential oil, if using. Transfer the mixture to a glass jar or tin. Let it cool completely before putting on the lid.

If using essential oils, try ones that have antimicrobial properties, such as patchouli, tea tree, or lavender, to increase the deodorant's effectiveness. If your body tends to get used to deodorants after wearing them for a while, meaning they simply stop working, switch up the essential oils with every batch to catch your underarm bacteria off guard.

To add more absorption power, replace one tablespoon of the arrowroot powder or cornstarch with a cosmetic clay. This will darken the color of the deodorant cream. To add more deodorizing power, replace one half to one tablespoon of the arrowroot powder or cornstarch with baking soda. Please note that baking soda can cause skin irritation in some people.

Apply the deodorant cream (a pea-sized amount for each underarm) to freshly washed skin or skin that has been thoroughly wiped with witch hazel astringent.

Side note: During the experimentation process I discovered that the too-oily deodorant cream I made first, which left oil marks on the underarms of my shirt, actually worked quite well as a moisturizing balm on my legs. Once it had fully absorbed my skin no longer felt oily at all. In fact, the arrowroot powder and kaolin clay in the formula gave it a sort of dry yet still moisturized feeling, which was quite a nice surprise.

Anatomy of a Balm

A balm, sometimes called a salve, is generally considered to be a spreadable substance, sometimes fragranced, used to soothe irritated skin. Most of the following balm recipes call for three ingredients: an oil, a butter, and a wax. However, a balm with two ingredients (i.e., a wax and an oil; a butter and an oil) works just as well. The consistency of the balm will vary with the ratio of ingredients used. Essential oils can be added for scent or to enhance the balm's healing properties.

To make a balm, melt the ingredients in the top of a double boiler. If using beeswax, put that in first as it will take the longest to melt. Add essential oils last, right before you pour the liquid into the tin or glass jar in which you want to store the balm. Wait until the balm has completely cooled before putting on the lid.

Makeup Remover Balm

I prefer to use heavy culinary oils for this balm as I think they do a better job than the skincare oils I've tried. Avocado oil in particular works well for my skin, but of course, use whatever oil you prefer.

Ingredients:

1.5 tablespoons beeswax

3 tablespoons shea butter

3 tablespoons cocoa butter

2 tablespoons oil

Yield: a little over ½ cup or 4.75 ounces

To use this balm, massage it gently over your face and closed eyes to loosen makeup and sunscreen. Remove the balm with warm water and a washcloth, then wash with your usual facial cleanser to make sure no traces of makeup, sunscreen, or balm are left behind.

Lip Balm

Try using the oil from the *Romantic Lip and Cheek Tint* recipe to make a rosy balm. It adds just a hint of color to the lips.

Ingredients:

2 teaspoons beeswax

2 teaspoons shea butter

2 teaspoons oil

Yield: 6 teaspoons or 2 tablespoons or 1 ounce

Aromatherapy Balm

This particular blend of scents was created to be calming, but of course you can use whichever essential oils you like for whatever purpose you need.

Ingredients:

1 teaspoon beeswax

1 teaspoon shea butter

1 teaspoon skincare oil

20 drops lavender

20 drops eucalyptus

10 drops bergamot (bergaptene-free, ideally, if using on skin)

Yield: 3 teaspoons or ½ ounce

To use this balm, dab a tiny bit of it under your nose or carry the tin around with you and take a sniff whenever you need it.

Lotion Bar

When I first tried to make a solid lotion bar I kept using beeswax, believing that's what made it solid. Strangely enough, the best way to make a solid balm is with no wax at all. The key is cocoa butter, which is hard at room temperature, but melts quickly when warmed up. The following recipe comes from the lovely book put out by Neal's Yard Remedies entitled *Essential Oils*. It calls for coconut oil, but you can use any culinary or skincare oil you like.

Ingredients:

2 tablespoons shea butter

2 tablespoons cocoa butter

1 tablespoon oil

10 drops essential oil (optional)

Yield: ¼ cup

This recipe can be used to make one large bar, or, as suggested in the book, several smaller ones. Try using paper cupcake wrappers, a metal muffin pan, an ice cube tray, or whatever else you have in the kitchen as a mold.

After you have poured the liquid balm mixture into your mold(s), let it cool to room temperature, which could take a few hours. If using a hard mold like a metal muffin pan, put it in the freezer for about an hour. Once the balm has frozen it should pop out of the mold when you turn it upside down and tap it against the counter. Paper cupcake wrappers can simply be peeled away from the balm before use. Place the balm(s) into a glass jar and store it in the fridge.

There are several ways to use this solid balm. Apply it to dry skin like lotion or use it on wet skin in the shower. Drop a small balm, or a piece of a larger one, into a warm bath to add moisturizing properties to the water.

Everyday Rituals

A ritual is a series of actions performed with special objects for a particular purpose. Although they are usually associated with religious or spiritual ceremonies, rituals can be created out of ordinary daily routines. In this section we will explore some ideas for simple, everyday rituals that support the wellbeing of the mind.

Practical Mysticism

We live in the space-time coordinates that we perceive in the gross physical plane, but we also live in a spaceless-timeless realm independent of the physical universe. Both mystics and physicists know this.

–Laurie Cabot, *Power of the Witch*

When casting spells, Witches use rituals and magical objects to amplify the energy of their intention as they send it into the metaphysical realm. As practical-minded kitchen witches, we can adapt some tools from Witchcraft—tarot cards, crystals, visualization—and use them in simple rituals to give us insight into ourselves and help us focus on our goals. The power resides not in the objects, but in the mind of the person working with them.

Tarot cards are traditionally used by fortune tellers to answer questions about a client's past, present, and future. To discover what the cards reveal about you, do a daily reading for yourself. Besides a deck of cards you will need a resource like a book or website that explains in detail the meaning of each card. In the morning or evening, shuffle the deck and either ask the cards for guidance about a specific issue or let them direct you to something they believe requires your attention. Then draw one card. Read about its meaning and consider how this applies to you. Interpreting the cards trains you to think in the language of symbols and archetypes. This allows you to see whatever you are asking the cards about from a different perspective, because you are processing information in a visual and abstract way, rather than with words and logic.

Let me illustrate how this can work. A few years ago I emailed my boss to ask for a (long overdue) raise. He welcomed the idea, but countered my suggestion for a specific amount with a lower number. It was tempting to just accept his offer and avoid prolonging an uncomfortable confrontation, but I decided not to respond until the next day. That night I called upon the tarot for help. After shuffling the deck, I turned over the top card to reveal the Emperor. Representing authority, logic, and strength, this guy would never accept anything less than what he believed he deserved. The cards knew exactly who I needed to talk to.

While trying to fall asleep that night, I imagined myself at a banquet table as a guest of the Emperor, and I asked him for advice. Though his wise words evaporated in the fog of a dream, they made an impression on my subconscious. In the morning I awoke with an unfamiliar sense of confidence, already composing my response email. In his reply later that day my boss agreed with my reasoning and gave me the original amount I had asked for. Honestly, without the Emperor's help I don't think I could have argued on my own behalf like that, but having done it once I can surely do it again.

Similar to tarot cards, crystals are both beautiful and unconventionally useful objects. Since ancient times, humans have believed that certain stones possess supernatural powers. Gaze into a crystal that contains the colors of the ethereal Aurora Borealis or glows softly like the moon and you will understand what captivated our ancestors. Despite resembling fragments of the night sky or alien worlds, these stones formed in the obscure depths of the Earth, some the result of comets and asteroids colliding into our infant planet. Consider what wisdom these minerals might contain, they who witnessed the Earth's formation.

But what can a rock actually do? Well, there is a crystal for pretty much any human problem. To find the right crystal for you, try one of the following two methods. First, you can visit a store that sells crystals (most likely a hippie shop that probably also has tarot cards) and buy the one that speaks to you. Read about its purported powers and contemplate what message this crystal, having convinced you to take it home, is trying to tell you. Alternatively, consult an expert source, such as Judy Hall's *The Crystal Bible*, and prescribe yourself a crystal to help you with a particular situation.

To help me focus during the workday I keep either a star ruby or mugglestone on top of my printer, where it peers down over my keyboard, willing me to keep typing. Whenever I glance up to take a break from the screen, there it is. Whether or not this little rock is emitting waves of energy, its presence alone reminds me why I placed it there and that I should get back to work. Another favorite stone is the chaorite, which sits on my nightstand because I have very vivid dreams whenever it's there. Is this merely a placebo effect? Probably. But the charoite's lovely purple and grey colors give it a rather soothing quality, perfect for something right next to a bed. Colors do affect our emotions and perhaps much of the appeal, and perhaps effectiveness, of crystals has something to do with that.

Of course, crystals work just as well outside the home. Katie likes to tuck a stone or two in her backpack to take with her as she goes through her day. A hunk of citrine, with its warm orange glow, has a way of imparting confidence and optimism. Sometimes she'll wear gemstones close to her body in the form of jewelry: She puts on her tiger's eye earrings whenever she needs clarity of mind.

However you work with tarot cards and crystals, which may or may not put you in touch with higher powers and ancient Earth energies, the process teaches you how to recognize your feelings and encourages you to better understand yourself in order to make improvements in your life. That's pretty powerful.

The Beauty of Sleep

Sleep that knits up the raveled sleave of care,
The death of each day's life, sore labor's bath,
Balm of hurt minds, great nature's second course,
Chief nourisher in life's feast.

—William Shakespeare, *Macbeth*

We all know that sleep is important. Just like good nutrition and exercise, sleep quite literally rebuilds our bodies and minds. No externally applied product can replicate what sleep does. If you tend to have trouble sleeping, creating a nighttime routine for yourself

The Dream Diary

The practice of kitchen witchery, as much as it is about connecting with nature, still treats the natural world as something outside of us. However, nature is *inside* of us, too. In order to strengthen our connection with the natural world, we can explore the wilderness of our subconscious.

All you need for an expedition through your mind is a notebook to record your observations. In other words, a dream diary. Every morning write down what happened while you slept. At first it may be difficult to remember much, but it becomes easier with practice. Revisit your entry in the evening and try to figure out what the dream was really about. There are plenty of books on dream symbolism that can offer clues to help you interpret your dreams, but it is probably more useful to take note of patterns in the themes and characters that show up frequently and figure out how

really helps, especially if you do it at the same time every day. Complete each step mindfully, focusing on the sensory experience. In this way a routine becomes a ritual to summon a restful sleep.

Taking a bath or shower in the evening creates a transition between day and night. Water, an ancient symbol of rebirth, washes away everything that happened in the previous hours, leaving your body and your mind clean and fresh. This helps to prevent any stress or negativity from following you to bed. However, if an evening shower or bath does not sound appealing, perhaps because you rely on your morning shower routine to start the day, try a footbath at night. To make a footbath, use a tub specifically designed for this purpose or a large mixing bowl or cooking pot.

Fill it with warm water and add a tablespoon or two of Epsom salt, a traditional remedy for sore muscles. There has been some confusion about whether the magnesium in Epsom salt, which can induce relaxation when taken as a supplement, is actually absorbed through the skin. Whether it can or not, just placing such a sensitive part of your body into warm water is itself quite calming.

Create a soothing ambiance throughout the evening by diffusing essential oils. This can be done via some kind of an essential oil diffuser or a room spray. Lavender is the classic option for a nighttime scent. Combine it with eucalyptus and peppermint to make your home smell clean and refreshed. For a more earthy, grounding scent try frankincense or patchouli.

Once you're finally all tucked in, rub a bit of a calming aromatherapy balm under your nose, or drop a bit of lavender essential oil on a tissue and place it on your pillow. Keep a crystal associated with sleep or dreams (i.e., moonstone, charoite, celestite) by your bed. Even if it doesn't actually emit any beneficial energy, whenever you see it you will remember that this is the time and place for sleep.

Creating a bedtime ritual, whatever that entails for you, is a way to reclaim a bit of time and space for yourself. A peaceful atmosphere and the comfort of a routine should help you relax in the evening, making falling asleep a bit easier. In the morning, fully recharged, you can resume bringing your particular magic to the world.

Conclusion

And there you have it, everything we know about kitchen witchery. Making things, working with the Earth, learning from our ancestors, and sharing ideas with our local communities—these are all things that connect us to a steady, stable force. Still, we could have never guessed when we first began working on our zine in the summer of 2016 just how much we would need this support in the years to come.

As a country we have lived through a most unprecedented presidency, when it felt like any day everything could fall down around us. As this book goes to press, we continue to slog through a pandemic. Life on Earth has never seemed so precious, so fragile but resilient at the same time. All these crises coming at us at once has given us a deep sense of compassion for our ancestors, for whom social, political, and religious upheaval—and a dash of plague here and there—was just to be expected. Sadly, in many parts of the world, this is still the case. We are reminded that our time here is brief, and that our lives are just a tiny part of the much greater history of humanity.

Throughout these tumultuous years we have spent a lot of time in our backyards and in the woods, taking comfort in knowing that, even when the human structures and systems around us seem to be under threat, we will always have a home in nature. Working on this book gave us a sense of purpose, just as looking after our homes, bodies, and loved ones always has. We hope its ideas will offer you the same feelings of support and comfort.

Remember, even when things get dark in the world, a lot of good can be created in your own kitchen.

Annotated Bibliography

Body Care

Ashenburg, Katherine. The Dirt On Clean: A Sanitized History. New York: North Point Press, 2007. A concise history on the role of bathing in western culture, from the Romans through today, which highlights how beliefs about health and hygiene have evolved over time. Water wasn't always considered good, and dirt wasn't always considered bad. This historical overview puts current trends into perspective.

Buc'hoz, Pierre-Joseph. The Toilet of Flora. London. 1779.This how-to book provides a fascinating insight into life in the late 18th century. While most of the recipes use obscure ingredients and solve problems we no longer have, the time travelling aspect of this work makes it worth a read. It is readily available for free online.

Grenville, Kate. The Case Against Fragrance. Melbourne, Australia: Text Publishing, 2017. Grenville is an Australian novelist who loved perfume until it started making her sick. As she tried to understand and manage her symptoms, she researched the fragrance industry and learned what ingredients are used in commercial perfumes and cleaners, the damage they can cause to our health, and the degree to which they are (or aren't) regulated.

Irene. "How To Make Herb-Infused Oils For Culinary And Body Care Use." Mountain Rose Herbs (blog). August 13, 2019. Accessed December 29, 2020. https://blog. mountainroseherbs.com/making-herbal-oils. This article provides an overview of the techniques used in infusing oils with herbs and details both the "folk method," which is our preference, and the quicker method, which requires the use of heat.

Michalun, M. Varinia, and Joseph C. Dinardo. Milady Skincare and Cosmetic Ingredients Dictionary. Clifton Park, New York: Milady, 2015. For those who wonder about what is actually in skincare and cosmetic products, this is a book worth reading. It is essentially a skincare primer that explains how skin works, what products can and cannot do, and includes a dictionary of common ingredients.

Moore, Ginger L. "Effective Use of Alcohol for Aromatic Blending." Tisserand Institute. November 7, 2017. Accessed June 3, 2019. tisserandinstitute.org/effective-use-alcohol-aromatic-blending/. The Tisserand Institute is a leading source of information on the safe use of essential oils, and this article is one of the very few we've found that clearly explains the importance of solubilizing essential oils before using them in air sprays.

Plummer, Beverly. Fragrance: How to Make Natural Soaps, Scents and Sundries. New York: Atheneum, 1975. This guide brings you straight back to the early 1970s in all their hippie glory. The spirit of this book, as well as many recipes, are as relevant as ever. Some recipes, however, are charmingly out of date. Most intriguing are the notes about ingredients, some of which seem exotic but apparently were available at the drugstore.

Essential Oils

Curtis, Susan, Pat Thomas, and Fran Johnson. Essential Oils: All-natural Remedies And Recipes For Your Mind, Body, And Home. New York: DK Publishing, 2016. A comprehensive and beautifully designed guide to essential oils, carrier oils, and aromatherapy from the experts at Neal's Yard Remedies, a renowned apothecary in Covent Garden, London. It includes lots of tips and recipes, and its full color photographs and smooth pages make it a pleasure to browse through.

Lail, Kristin. "Everclear 101: Essential Oils and Everclear." Plant Therapy (blog). June 28, 2019. Accessed July 31, 2019. blog.planttherapy.com/blog/2019/06/28/everclear-101-essential-oils/. Lail's article spells out the basics on solubilizing essential oils with grain alcohol.

Worwood, Valerie Ann. The Complete Book of Essential Oils and Aromatherapy. Novato, CA: New World Library, 2016. This hefty tome is an extensive reference guide to everything about essential oils, from their use in aromatherapy to skincare and general health. Detailed tables outlining the most important information makes finding what you need quick and easy. We used this book to find safety indications on the essential oils we recommend.

Gardening and Plants

Amberson, Joshua James et al. Growing Things: A Guide for Beginning Gardeners. Portland, OR: Self-published zine, 2012. This lovely zine is filled with advice for the novice gardener. More than anything we appreciate its attitude and approach toward gardening: namely, that it doesn't need to be too complicated or fussily planned.

BC Wolverton; WL Douglas; K Bounds. "Interior landscape plants for indoor air pollution abatement." NASA, September 1989. This is the report from the NASA Clean Air Study that looks at how plants purify the air indoors. Updates were made to the study in the '90s that include additional plants. The entire report is available for public use on NASA's website.

Beston, Henry. Herbs And The Earth. Boston: David R. Godine, 1990. Although it contains some practical information, this little book is really a poetic homage to plants and gardening.

Boland, Maureen & Bridget. Gardeners' Lore: Plantings, Potions and Practical Wisdom. Hopewell, NJ: The Ecco Press, 1998. The Boland sisters kept a garden in London and later in the countryside in Hampshire from the 1930s to the 1970s, when this book was originally published. This charming book is just what it sounds like: gardening tips with legend and lore braided in.

Coyne, Kelly and Erik Knutzen. The Urban Homestead. Port Townsend, WA: Process Media, 2010. This book is brimming with instructions on doing down-home stuff in the city, from growing your own food to keeping livestock. We find its practical attitude about composting especially useful.

Dumont, Henrietta. The Language of Flowers: The Floral Offering: A Token of Affection and Esteem, Comprising the Language and Poetry of Flowers. Philadelphia: H.C. Peck & T. Bliss, 1853. This cool Victorian-era book gives the symbolic meaning ascribed to dozens of flowers and other plants by the English and Americans, and includes poems and passages relating to each one.

Haegele, Liz. "Composting." Garden Seeds Blog of the Scott Arboretum. February 25, 2008. Accessed November 4, 2019. www.scottarboretum.org/composting/. This helpful article provides information on composting for people who live in apartments.

Lawson, Nancy. The Humane Gardener. New York: Princeton Architectural Press, 2017. More than just useful gardening tips, this book offers hope that if we all take control of our backyards and return them to a more natural state, we can heal at least some of the damage human civilization has wrought on our local ecosystems. More information and resources are available on the companion website: www.humanegardener.com

NYC Compost Project. "Compost Made Easy." August 2016. Accessed June 2019. earthmatter. org/wp-content/uploads/2016/08/tip-sheet-compost-made-easy-cpts-spez-f.pdf. The NYC Compost Project is an excellent resource for beginning composters, particularly those living in small or urban spaces. They have published several "tip sheets" like this one, and all of them can be accessed for free on Earth Matter NY's website.

Simmons, Adelma Grenier. Herb Gardening in Five Seasons. New York: E.P. Dutton, 1964. Written in the 60s by someone who was old-fashioned at the time, Herb Gardening in Five Seasons is packed with arcane knowledge on the pagan holidays, as well as advice for growing and using herbs throughout the year. (The fifth season is Christmas.)

Sparrow. "Small Happiness." The Sun, July 2015. This beautiful essay by the poet Sparrow is not really about gardening, but it contains the most gorgeous description of composting that we've ever read.

Herbalism

Breverton, Terry. Breverton's Complete Herbal: A Book Of Remarkable Plants And Their Uses. Guilford, Connecticut: Lyons Press, 2011. An expanded version of Culpeper's Herbal. It includes uses for the modern herbalist, as well as some historical tidbits about a few of the plants, which makes for a well-rounded guide that's useful as well as fun to read.

Culpeper, Nicholas. Culpeper's Color Herbal. New York: Sterling Pub Co., 2002. This edition of Culpeper's groundbreaking 1649 herbal presents his original text, which details information about hundreds of herbs, alongside current usage advice for each entry.

Davidow, Joie. Infusions of Healing: A Treasure of Mexican-American Herbal Remedies. New York: Fireside, 1999. Davidow is a journalist who spent years learning both the history of plant healing in ancient Mexico and the way plants are used by Mexican people today to treat a huge range of ailments. Beautiful book.

Giglio, Frank. "How to Make Herbal Vinegar." *Mountain Rose Herbs* (blog). October 1, 2018. blog.mountainroseherbs.com/how-to-make-herbal-vinegar. This is one of many useful how-to articles on the Mountain Rose Herbs website.

Mitchem, Stephanie. African American Folk Healing. New York: New York University Press, 2007. Mitchem's book looks at the origins of traditional African American remedies and rituals, as well as the cultural meaning they have for Black Americans today.

Sherrow, Jo-Jo. Healing Your Magical Body with Plants. Self-published zine, 2011. This zine consists primarily of medicinal herbal advice. Sherrow's information on steeping times for the different parts of a plant when making herbal infusions was useful to us for this book.

Stuart, Malcolm, Ed. The Encyclopedia of Herbs and Herbalism. New York: Crescent Books, 1979. This book is a wealth of knowledge on everything you might want to know about herbs, from growing them to eating them to using them as medicine.

Thulesius, Olav. Nicholas Culpeper. New York: St. Martin's Press, 1992. This relatively short but thorough book about Culpeper's life and work includes photographs of the buildings where Culpeper and his family lived or worshipped and illustrations from his Herbal.

Ward, Beth. "The Long Tradition of Folk Healing Among Southern Appalachian Women." Atlas Obscura. November 21, 2017. Accessed December 9, 2019. www.atlasobscura.com/articles/southern-appalachia-folk-healers-granny-women-neighbor-ladies. Ward's article looks at the history and culture of Appalachian folk healing, sometimes known as folk magic.

History

Ehrenreich, Barbara and Deirdre English. Witches, Midwives & Nurses: A History of Women Healers. New York: Feminist Press, 2010. A piece of Second Wave feminist history, this book recounts the role of women in medicine throughout the ages, which at the time of its first printing in 1973 was a radical undertaking.

Folkard, Richard. Plant Lore, Legends, and Lyrics: Embracing the Myths, Traditions, Superstitions, and Folk-lore of the Plant Kingdom. London: Sampson, Low, Marston, 1892. Folkard collected thousands of legends about the magical uses of plants from around the world, from ancient times to his present day in the 19th century.

Woolley, Benjamin. The Herbalist: Nicholas Culpeper and the Fight for Medical Freedom. London: HarperCollins, 2004. Culpeper is a preeminent figure in the history of herbal knowledge, having authored a seminal herbal for the common person. In this biography we learn about the social, political, and religious upheavals of his time (the period of the English Civil War), which feel strangely familiar to us today.

Household

Gruenberg, Louise. Herbal Home Hints. Emmaus, PA: Rodale Press, 1999. This is one of the best books we've seen on the subject of natural cleaning. Gruenberg provides many household recipes that call for a variety of ingredients, including but not limited to essential oils. She also includes diagrams of herb garden layouts and a table of natural ingredients that describes their characteristics, uses, and places where they can be purchased.

"How Toxic Are Your Household Cleaning Supplies?" Organic Consumers Association. Accessed April 15, 2019. www.organicconsumers.org/news/how-toxic-are-your-household-cleaning-supplies. How toxic indeed!

"Making Natural Dyes From Plants." Pioneer Thinking (blog). June 29, 2012. Accessed November 29, 2019. https://pioneerthinking.com/natural-dyes. This article provided us with the basics on natural fabric dyeing. It also gives a long list of plants you can use to achieve different colors.

Moss, Doug and Scheer, Roddy. "Avoid Harsh Chemicals in Commercial Air Fresheners with Homemade Alternatives." Scientific American. September 9, 2012. Accessed November 4, 2019. www.scientificamerican.com/article/nontoxic-air-fresheners/. This article reports on the dangerous effects some chemicals in commercial air fresheners can have on our health.

Normandeau, Sheryl. "Fall Cleaning Hacks with Herbs," The Herb Quarterly. San Ramon, CA:EGW Publishing, Fall 2016. The Herb Quarterly has been in print for more than 40 years and is useful for both novice and experienced herbal hobbyists. It's also very pretty. This article alone gave us several new ideas for house cleaning with herb plants and other natural ingredients.

Peltier, Karen. "Vinegar for Green Cleaning," The Spruce. thespruce.com/vinegar-definition-green-cleaning-uses-1707034. It's amazing how much you can do around the house with vinegar.

Rapinchuk, Becky. The Organically Clean Home. Avon, MA: Adams Media, 2014. This book contains a great many useful recipes for household cleaning—and it's the one that started Katie on her natural house-cleaning journey. Rapinchuk keeps a blog at cleanmama.net.

"Signaling Science: What Household Solutions Repel Ants?" Scientific American. Accessed November 4, 2019. www.scientificamerican.com/article/bring-science-home-ant-solution. This simple, useful article, written for children, explains the science behind ant behavior.

Siegel-Maier, Karyn. The Naturally Clean Home. Pownal, VT: Storey Publishing, ebook version 2015. This pretty book contains many tips on keeping your household clean and healthy. It also contains detailed information on the germ-killing properties of many essential oils.

Wildcrafting

Berry, Rachel. "Safe and Ethical Guidelines for Wildcrafting." *Sierra Botanica* (blog). January 20, 2015. Accessed September 30, 2019. sierrabotanica.com/2015/01/safe-ethical-guidelines-for-wildcrafting/. The author provides a handy list of ways that beginning foragers can harvest wild plants sustainably.

"The Foraging Course." Herbal Academy. 24 South Road, Bedford, MA 01730. theherbalacademy.com. The Herbal Academy offers online herbalism courses, articles, and monographs. This (paid) course covers the basics of foraging plants for use in cooking and medicinal preparations. It also goes over ethics and conservation.

Fritsch, Al and Gallimore, Paul. Healing Appalachia: Sustainable Living through Appropriate Technology. Lexington, KY: University of Kentucky Press, 2007. The chapter on wildcrafting provided us with some background on the subject and advice on how to do it responsibly.

Klenner, Amanda. "Wildcrafting Ethics." The Herbarium. Accessed November 24, 2019. herbarium.theherbalacademy.com/2015/09/wildcrafting-ethics/ Klenner

is a clinical herbalist who discusses the ethics of foraging plants in the wild.

Witchcraft and Esoterica

Cabot, Laurie. Power of the Witch. New York: Delta, 1989. Cabot, designated the Official Witch of Salem by the governor of Massachusetts in 1977, explains her philosophy of magic and provides practical instructions for spells and the like.

Hall, Judy. The Crystal Bible. Cincinnati, OH: Walking Stick Press, 2003. This is a small but thick little book filled with detailed descriptions and full color photographs of so many kinds of crystals. But it does not include them all. If you can't find a particular crystal in this book, try one of the other two in this series.

Tea, Michelle. Modern Tarot. New York: HarperCollins, 2017. Tea breaks down the meaning of the cards' symbolism in great detail, from her queer, radical, and frequently hilarious perspective. If you're interested in a take on Tarot that breaks through the gender binary, this is the book for you. In her introduction, Tea shares her thoughts about the recent rise of interest in witchcraft and traditional wisdom.

Resources

Aura Cacia makes essential oils and carrier oils as well as natural skincare products. They are often sold in natural food stores, but some drugstores and conventional grocery stores carry a selection as well. Their website, where you can buy all of their products as well as containers to store your creations, features a whole section devoted to DIY skincare recipes. Auracacia. com

Bulk Apothecary is a large online catalog of items used in homemade personal care products, sold in bulk and at a discount. We recommend it for tools such as dark-colored glass bottles, different types of spray nozzles, and tubes and tins for balms. Bulkapothecary.com

The Herbarium is an online educational resource. Created by the Herbal Academy, which offers online courses in herbalism, this inexpensive annual membership gives you access to articles and other media that will enhance your herbal education. We found the articles on wildcrafting and herbal preparations, such as infusions and tinctures, especially useful. Theherbalacademy.com

The Herbiary sells herbs, teas, tonics, and many other "supplies for sacred living." They carry the Pranarom line of essential oils and hydrosols, which are made from sustainably-harvested, organic plants. The shop has locations in Philadelphia's Reading Terminal Market and in Asheville, North Carolina, and you can order products from the website. Herbiary.com

Your Local Library probably has many of the books in the bibliography, and more. In fact, that's where we found most of them!

Mountain Rose Herbs is a reputable mail-order and online retailer of high-quality, certified organic essential oils and pretty much any ingredient or tool you might need for your witchy projects. It was founded in 1987 by herbalist Rosemary Gladstar. The website is also an excellent source of informative articles on how to use them. Mountainroseherbs.com

The National Garden Clubs, Inc. is the umbrella organization of local garden clubs across the U.S. It is an excellent source of education, community, and even scholarships and grant opportunities. Gardenclub.org

The Old Farmer's Almanac might be the single best resource available for gardening, astronomy, and weather information. Its annual almanac has been in print since 1792, and it now exists as a website and email newsletter too. Almanac.com

Seedsavers Exchange is a nonprofit organization that sells seeds for herbs, flowers, and vegetables, focusing on heirloom varieties. But they don't just sell seeds! As the name implies, they run an exchange program that allows people to find and share seeds. Seedsavers.org

The Spruce is a website that offers environmentally conscious, DIY approaches to house cleaning, home decor, gardening, and more. They also explain the science behind the recipes and ingredients they recommend. Thespruce.com

The Tisserand Institute was founded by Robert Tisserand in London in 1988. Tisserand is the author of *Essential Oil Safety*, a book that is considered an industry standard. The Tisserand

Institute provides educational information on the proper use of essential oils, based on clinical evidence and research, in the form of paid online courses and free articles on its website.

Tisserandinstitute.org

Credits

Macbeth from Folger Digital Texts, ed. Barbara Mowat, Paul Werstine, Michael Poston, and Rebecca Niles. Folger Shakespeare Library. Accessed on December 11, 2019. www.folgerdigitaltexts.org

Romeo and Juliet from Folger Digital Texts, ed. Barbara Mowat, Paul Werstine, Michael Poston, and Rebecca Niles. Folger Shakespeare Library. Accessed on December 11, 2019. www.folgerdigitaltexts.org

Liz Haegele, who discussed air-purifying houseplants with us, is Katie's sister. She owns Fine Garden Creations, a garden design company in the Delaware Valley. Visit the company's website at www.finegardencreations.com for a blog that's chock-full of gardening advice and information on specific plants.

Helen Kaucher makes all kinds of art under the name Hels' Bells Handmade. She's also a professional baker and helps run her family's farm and stand, where they grow and sell 320 varieties of tomato from seed. Hels kindly gave us some tips on dyeing fabric with plant material.

Melba is the magical human who gave Katie her first jar of homemade laundry soap. She makes gorgeous jewelry out of copper and other metals, animal bones, and stones, many of which she finds in the woods. Follow her on Instagram @ waxleaf and visit her online shop at www.etsy.com/shop/WaxLeaf.

Melissa Manna is the Philadelphia-based crafter who kindly shared her instructions for making beeswax kitchen wraps with us. She creates all kinds of things, from deodorant to Christmas gifts, and she especially loves using fabrics and supplies that belonged to her mother when she was young. To see Melissa's projects and find out when she'll be leading a workshop, follow her on Instagram @melissajmanna.

ABOUT US

Katie

I'm a writer, mainly of creative nonfiction and essays. I have also published a memoir called *White Elephants*; a collection of essays about language called *Slip of the Tongue*; and a book of stories called *Cats I've Known*. (Yes, they are all stories about cats.) I have also written for the Philadelphia Inquirer, the Utne Reader, Bitch, Adbusters, the Millions, and many other magazines.

As for what led me to write this book, the early influence of my family was pretty important. I grew up in a home where making things with your hands was valued and encouraged. My mother taught me to knit and do embroidery, and as a young adult I learned to sew on her heavy old sewing machine. Her father, my Pop, could build anything, from the bows he used for hunting to the kiln he used to fire his pottery. My sister Liz and I watched our parents grow vegetables and herbs in their backyard gardens every summer, and today Liz is a professional gardener who gives me information and help (and plants!) when I need them. And my dad, who grew up playing in the woods of Philadelphia's enormous Fairmount Park, taught me how to hike safely, row a canoe decently, and bait a fish hook without being a baby about it.

I have German, Irish, English, and Jewish ancestry. There are surely plenty of other things mixed in there too, but those are the backgrounds that found their way into my family culture, belief system, and customs. I was raised Catholic and was deeply pleased when, as a teenager, I began to understand that many of the traditions I'd grown up with were actually nature-based, pre-Christian practices. The symbolism in those ancient traditions has always felt right to me, and some of my most significant and joyous experiences of healing and connection have come about through my practice of nature-based spirituality.

Today I live in an old residential Philadelphia neighborhood, just a few miles from the house I grew up in. I live with my husband Joe, an artist who happens to be a really good gardener and cook. His help was invaluable to me as I tinkered with the recipes for this book. Together he and I publish zines, make music, and host shows, and we are proud to be a part of the city's vibrant, scrappy, and beautifully queer community of artists. In that same spirit, much of the information in this book is communal knowledge. It has always been shared among friends and family and passed down through the generations. I'm an imperfect, non-expert, enthusiastic participant in traditions that have been around for a very long time.

Nadine

My life began in Germany, and the first stories I ever heard featured witches and magic. After the death of my father, my mother and I left our neat German suburb for the quasi-wilderness of New England. Ghosts of the first English settlers and Native Americans lurked in the woods around my house, most palpably on autumn days when the scent of smoke from the neighbor's chimney mingled with a grey mist. I spent many hours playing among the trees, following the stream that flowed through them as far as I dared.

But nature was not just a playground to me. The more I learned about it, the more responsibility I felt to protect it. The passion of my teachers, who made environmental education part of every year's curriculum, probably had a lot to do with that. My classmates and I went on field trips to orchards, farms, forests, and our town's nature center. In junior high we spent a week by the ocean, studying the creatures that live in tidepools. There is no way I could have grown up in this community without developing a deep respect for the natural world.

Browsing around a bookstore one summer during high school I discovered *Power of the Witch* by Laurie Cabot. It contained a mix of history, feminism,

Witchcraft fundamentals, and an intriguing theory about energy. For about a year I worked on casting spells. Although I eventually stopped dabbling in Witchcraft, my love for the idea of magic never waned.

Today, the work I do for a television production company that creates educational shows for children has given me access to current research in many different fields of science. It is remarkable what humans have been able to accomplish and what will be possible in the near future. All of this would look like pure sorcery to our ancestors, though I wonder if they knew things that we have yet to rediscover.

At my house in the greater Philadelphia area, where I live with my boyfriend Tim and an Australian shepherd, I try to make our small rectangle of suburban land a healthy piece of the greater ecosystem. The look of the neighborhood is distinctly American, but sometimes when I'm taking a walk around it the sight of an evergreen tree, positioned in a very particular way in front of a brick house, transports me right back to the German suburb I left as a child. In these moments I remember that no matter where any of us are on this planet, we are always home.